C000299454

ENCOUNTER
WITH
GOD
IN
1 CORINTHIANS

ENCOUNTER
WITH
GOD
IN
1 CORINTHIANS

MORGAN DERHAM

SERIES EDITORS
ALISON BARR, JOSEPHINE CAMPBELL, TONY HOBBS

SCRIPTURE UNION

Scripture Union, 207–209 Queensway, Bletchley MK2 2EB, England.

© Morgan Derham 1996

First published 1996

ISBN 1 85999 042 8

All rights reserved. No part of this publication may be reproduced, stored in a retrieval system, or transmitted, in any form or by any means, electronic, mechanical, photocopying, recording or otherwise, without the prior permission of Scripture Union.

The right of Morgan Derham to be identified as author of this work has been asserted by him in accordance with the Copyright, Designs and Patents Act 1988.

Unless otherwise attributed, Scripture quotations are taken from the Holy Bible, New International Version. Copyright © 1973, 1978, 1984 by International Bible Society. Anglicisation copyright © 1979, 1984, 1989. Used by permission of Hodder and Stoughton Limited.

British Library Cataloguing-in-Publication Data
A catalogue record for this book is available from the British Library.

Cover design and illustration by Grax Design Consultants.

Printed and bound in Great Britain by Cox & Wyman Ltd, Reading.

CONTENTS

FOREWORD

Throughout its long history, promoting systematic daily Bible reading has always been central to Scripture Union's worldwide ministry. At first there were Bible-reading cards that detailed a series of daily readings throughout the year. But before too long comments were published to accompany the notes and, in the early 1920s, a quarterly booklet was produced. It was called *The Scripture Union* with the sub-title 'Daily Notes', the name by which the booklet was to become known.

By the 1990s Scripture Union's promotion of systematic daily Bible reading relied on three separate Bible-reading notes for the English-speaking world. Like *Daily Notes*, *Daily Bread* was widely used over several decades, and these two were joined more recently by *Alive To God* which was launched to offer a complementary approach to Bible reading. All three publications have always had the following in common:

- A commitment to the authority and inspiration of biblical text;
- A conviction that reading the Bible should not be merely a cerebral process: the reader should also be encouraged to respond to what they have read.

Bible-reading notes inevitably reflect the culture and concerns of their time. So, for example, some of the early notes made frequent attempts to summarise biblical passages using three points. Although this was a useful *aide-mémoire*, it did tend to be somewhat forced at times! More interestingly, the notes of the '30s, '40s and '50s – when the evangelical world was struggling with the impact of the implications of liberal scholarship – concentrated on re-stating the basic doctrinal truths. Today the notes reflect a strong emphasis on the importance of applying biblical principles and the growing interest throughout the Christian world on what can be described as 'spirituality'. This is seen in the increasingly varied forms of worship, the rediscovery of ancient Christian writing and music, and an awareness that responding to God can involve feelings and emotions as well as the mind.

There is much in Christian culture that is exciting and refreshing, but it is taking place against a background of a widespread decrease in Bible reading. It seems that the emphasis on Christian experience – important as that is – is blinding many people to the other side of the Christian life: duty and discipline. Twenty years ago most members of evangelical churches were committed to the importance of personal Bible reading on a regular basis. Nowadays, although many churches would claim to be Bible based, individual members have all too often given up regular personal Bible reading. Bible-reading aids cannot in themselves change this trend. What we must continue to pray for is God's Holy Spirit to provoke whole Christian communities to rediscover the importance and excitement of regular Bible reading – without losing the joy of the variety and depth of Christian experience.

Marrying regular Bible reading with dynamic Christian experience is the aim of Scripture Union's Bible-reading notes. Partly to reflect this principle, it was recently decided to change the title of *Daily Notes* to *Encounter With God*. The former described the process but the latter describes the purpose.

Over the years readers have often encouraged us to reprint popular series of the notes. However, we have always been reluctant to do so, partly because writers prepare notes prayerfully and under the guidance of the Holy Spirit for use at a particular time and in a particular way. Numerous stories from readers testify to how a particular note on a particular day met a specific need, and are witnesses to the Holy Spirit's role in the process. Nevertheless, when in the early 1990s we began to deal with entire biblical books in a single series, a formula began to suggest itself: not a reprinting of the series as such, but the series re-worked and expanded by the writer; still using the distinctive *Encounter With God* approach, but with the space to develop and explore some of the issues which could not be covered in a 300-word note.

There are a number of things that make Scripture Union Bible-reading notes distinctive, but one element perhaps stands out above all others: beginning and ending with scripture. Starting with the Bible passage, the writer offers thought-provoking comments to encourage the reader to go back to the passage with fresh enthusiasm and new insights, eager to respond with new commitment to what God is saying through scripture: in other words, *to encounter God*. It is the prayer of all who have worked on this series that such will be your experience as you read this book.

Tony Hobbs, Publishing Co-ordinator

INTRODUCTION

The existence of the church at Corinth was a miracle: the condition of the church at Corinth was a scandal.

We need to appreciate this apparent contradiction if we want to get to the heart of this extraordinary Bible book. This is no theological treatise or learned study of 'Christianity in Romano-Greek culture', though there is much important doctrine in what Paul has written and it reveals a great deal about the world of its day. Instead, here is a warm, lively, human document, written at white heat and full of deep feeling. Moreover, Paul gives practical advice on very modern issues – issues like marriage, divorce, sexual behaviour, inter-faith relationships, the role of women in the church, the resurrection, famine-relief funds, leadership in the church, charismatic worship and the right understanding of Communion. The first letter to the Corinthians is very much a living document, relevant to human life in any age, not just an interesting bit of history.

To take one example: religious pluralism is a hot topic in Britain and elsewhere today. The Christian church has to live and witness in communities where Christianity no longer has a virtual monopoly and where it is challenged by powerful rival faiths and systems of belief. This was exactly the situation in which the New Testament church found itself – there were hundreds of sects around the Mediterranean rim including, in particular, the official Roman religion which deified the Caesars in a powerful blend of political and religious imperialism. Pluralism was the way of life for the citizens of Corinth, and Christianity only a small, minority religion in comparison.

> The transition, then, from the way in which the biblical authors thought about the world, with all of its religious pluralism, to how we should think about ours, with all of its competing religious claims, is shorter, less complex, and easier than it has been for centuries. Indeed, it involves no transition at all.
>
> (From *No Place for Truth,* David Wells, Eerdmans [US], 1993, p 264.)

Indeed, the culture of sophisticated, cosmopolitan Corinth was hostile to Christianity. The claims of Christ cut across much of the accepted way of life in the city, where paganism aimed its appeal directly at basic human instincts – sensuality, greed, pride and the glorification of the human body. As one ancient writer put it:

> In the young pagan world
> Men deified the beautiful, the glad,
> The strong, the boastful, and it came to nought.
> We have raised pain and sorrow into heaven.
>
> (Athelwold)

All this had an effect on the church. Many new converts were finding it hard to leave behind their old way of life and follow in the steps of Christ:

> Might they not watch the temple women dance at some lovely festival in the temple of Acrocorinth? Were they henceforth to gaze, in dreaming fantasy, not upon bright faces of youthful deities, garlanded with rose and hyacinth, but on the marred visage of the One who was crowned with thorns? It was hard to curb and crucify passions which once they had consecrated under the name of religion.
>
> (Dean Farrar)

Corinth was a flourishing trade centre, a Roman colony with an above average proportion of Roman citizens, a focus for athleticism – the Isthmian Games were held nearby – and for pagan idolatry. Starting in the Forum, a visitor taking a tour of the city in Paul's day would see first the temples of Demeter and Persephone, Artemis, Dionysius then, nearby, those of Octavia, Apollo and Hera Acraia; moving out from the Forum, he would encounter temples and statues dedicated to Poseidon, Hermes, Zeus, Aphrodite, Aesculapius, Isis, Melaenis and Heracles.* Commercialism, luxury and licentiousness dominated city life. In Greek drama if a drunkard or a lecher appeared on stage it was assumed he was a Corinthian, and vice versa.

So it was that the existence of a church in the midst of such a corrupt community was indeed miraculous – a fact that Paul used to vindicate his claim to be an apostle (1 Cor 9:1–2). The paradox that this church was also in a disgraceful state should not surprise us – it is a reflection of the inner contradictions experienced by the Christian church in all places and at all times, including our own.

It is worth asking what kind of picture of the New Testament church we might have had if Paul had not written this epistle. There are hints of blemishes here and there in other accounts of the early church (eg Acts 6:1; Gal 2:11–13; 3:1–3; Phil 4:1–3), but it would have been easy to idealise the first Christians, as some have done. 1 Corinthians pulls aside the curtain and reveals a church with many faults and failures, struggling in the wake of the negative influences exerted on it by the culture to which it belonged. But Paul's letter also reveals the Holy Spirit at work, countering the incursions of the enemy and opening the way for truly Christlike living. As we shall see in his opening remarks, in spite of all its failures Paul regarded the Corinthian church as God's handiwork and gave no hint of wanting to write it off or start again.

To help us get the 'feel' of 1 Corinthians, and to catch something of Paul's mood as he wrote, we begin with an imagined reconstruction of how he received the missive from Corinth that prompted him to write in the first place.

We shall get an idea of how he set about dealing with the true needs of the church, which their letter to him had carefully avoided mentioning. Let your imagination get to work as you read. Feel something of the passion in Paul's heart as he agonised over the community that had come to mean so much to him. Open your heart as well as your mind to the prompting of the Spirit who inspired Paul's response.

* (Note to p 13) Information source: the *Tyndale Bulletin* 42:2, Bruce Winter, p 210, with the help of Pausanius who wrote a kind of contemporary tourist guide to Corinth.

A LETTER AND A MEETING

'A letter for you, Paul, from Corinth. It came while you were out visiting Tyrannus' academy. The people who brought it have gone to find lodgings in the city, but they said they would be back to see you tomorrow.'

At the mention of Corinth, the small, rather bent, sun-burnt man looked up sharply and reached for the scroll held out to him. 'From Corinth!' he said eagerly. 'I've been looking forward to hearing their news.' But then he hesitated. 'My eyes are troubling me more than usual today. Would you read it to me, Gaius, my brother?'

His companion sat down beside the apostle at the heavy wooden table on which there was an array of reed pens, iron styli, ink bottles and papyri. This was where the apostle did most of his thinking, writing, planning and praying over the infant churches he had established all over the Mediterranean region. Gaius broke the seal, unrolled the scroll and began to read.

'Greetings in the Lord to our beloved Paul, from the elders of the church of Jesus Christ at Corinth. We remember you in all we do, and we thank God for your ministry among us.

'We continue to try hard to hold firmly to all the things you taught us when you first revealed the riches of God's grace in Jesus Christ. We are grateful to God for his many blessings, and for the progress we have made as a church in the three years since you were last here. We appreciated your warning when you last wrote to us that we should not have too much to do with those who have deviated from the true path but, as you know, it is not easy in a city like Corinth to follow such advice too strictly. Nevertheless, we will keep what you say in mind.

'However, there are some matters relating to difficulties that have recently arisen in the church, on which we would like your advice. Some among us felt that perhaps we should also seek a resolution on these questions from the church leaders in Jerusalem who, because they were with the Lord when he was alive, may have better insight as to what his word on these issues might be. However, as our founder we still value your advice and hope that you will be able to throw some light on the problem.'

Paul broke in: 'So! They want to throw aside my authority over them as an apostle and only seek my advice. But ... carry on, Gaius.'

'The matter of marriage is causing some trouble just now: it seems to have generated a great deal of controversy. We have people in the church who are not sure if they should get married at all. Sexual intercourse is such a major part of the ceremonies that go on in the pagan temples around us – shouldn't we avoid it altogether in order to live holy and pure lives, as the Lord no doubt intended that we should? As for those who were already married before they became Christians, wouldn't it be better to give up all that and live a celibate life together as sister and brother before the Lord? And shouldn't women whose husbands have died remain free of marital ties and so avoid being contaminated by sexual impurity?

'There is one particularly tricky question – if a husband or wife becomes a Christian but their spouse does not, must they stay together, bound to an unbeliever for the rest of their lives? Should those in the church who are fathers go on trying to arrange marriages for their daughters? Shouldn't they rather encourage them to live as virgins, which seems to many of us much the better way?'

Gaius paused here, wondering what Paul was making of all this. But the apostle made no comment as he mulled over what he had heard. Then he nodded to Gaius to continue.

'Some of us, particularly those in business, have found ourselves facing a dilemma when we are invited out to dine with friends who are not members of the church. These meals frequently take place in a temple and, as you will know, the meat that is eaten will have been offered as a sacrifice to the resident god or goddess. Now *we* know, as you taught us so thoroughly, that an idol is a complete nonentity – there is only the one, true and living God whom we worship. So offerings made to idols are meaningless and there is no reason why we should not go along. We remember you saying how we needed to keep in touch with all kinds and conditions of people so that we can impart the gospel to them and thus save some of them. It does help our business folk to be able to go to these dinner parties, especially those who are members of the trade guilds which arrange them. And we must not forget our poorer members, who rarely get a treat like the meat that is given away after the temple feasts.'

Paul nodded. 'That's a difficult one, I agree. I'm glad they have remembered what I said about not losing touch with people outside the church. But I hope they also remember what I said about not being the cause of others losing their faith.'

Gaius continued: 'There are people in the church who came to it from the synagogue in which you first preached here. They are worried because women are taking an active part in our meetings nowadays. And, what is more, these women don't always wear a head-covering as they did when you were with us, and the Jewish members want us to insist that they do. But we don't feel that this is an important enough issue to cause an upset over, and some of these women are very eloquent – their ministry is a blessing. After all, a large proportion of the church don't come from a Jewish background and, as we are now a new people in Christ, why should we be bound by the traditions of the Jewish community?

'Meetings are going very well. A good number of people actually take part, and there is a lively feeling of worship.

17

But we do sometime have difficulties with those who want to speak in mysterious "tongues", like the priests in the temples around us. We can get two or three on their feet at a time, all speaking or prophesying simultaneously. It is difficult to make out what each of them is saying, and several people have complained that when they have brought newcomers to the meetings, these visitors were put off by the noise and confusion. But if God is speaking through those people, we can't stifle them, can we?'

Paul shook his head. 'I don't like the sound of that at all,' he said. 'Those Corinthians always did have a tendency to give free play to their emotions, especially the Greeks among them, and they are rather too anxious to make an impression.'

Gaius grunted in agreement.

'Some of the better educated members are having difficulties with your teaching about the resurrection. The Greek members believe in life after death, but they can't understand why we have to believe that our bodies are going to be resurrected or even why Jesus appeared again in a body after he had risen. One of them talks about the business of the empty tomb being unnecessary to faith. Isn't it enough to know that Jesus is living on in the Spirit among us?'

Paul frowned. 'Now, this I shall have to deal with thoroughly!' he said grimly. 'The resurrection is fundamental to following Jesus in the Way! All their faith becomes useless if they jettison it. How could they be tripped up over such a basic matter of faith?'

'We are sorry to trouble you with these minor matters. On the whole, we think the work is very encouraging and, once again, we must thank you for all that you did in giving the church such a solid foundation. Those of us who have become believers since you left are especially keen to meet you. You have been away from us for such a long time now and have not even allowed us to contribute to your ministry, as many of us would have liked to do. But perhaps you feel that such support is unwarranted.

'Once again, we greet you, along with Gaius and the others in Ephesus: from your brothers in the church of Jesus Christ in Corinth.'

Gaius rolled up the scroll and placed it on the table, all the while glancing at his friend to gauge how this news had affected him. Paul sat with bowed shoulders, his eyes worried as he contemplated what he had heard. Then, suddenly, he thumped the table, sending ink bottles and pens scattering.

'"Minor matters", eh?! I wish they were. "Things are encouraging"? I can't imagine a church in a worse condition! Everything I taught them, vanishing like the mist. Gaius, what can be done? We will have to work fast to stop this kind of rot. I can hardly bear to hear what news our visitors will bring tomorrow.'

Paul rose quickly to greet the three men who arrived the following morning.

'Stephanas, dear brother, one of the first at Corinth to choose to follow Christ. Welcome in the name of the Lord!' He threw his arms around the leader of the group and kissed his cheek. 'It is indeed good to see you again!' he went on. 'I trust you had a pleasant journey to Ephesus. And you too, Fortunatus. How are things with Chloe? Are you still in her service? And who is this you have brought with you?'

Fortunatus drew his other travelling companion into the circle. 'This is Achaicus. He joined Chloe's household two years ago and has since become a believer. He came with us because besides our visit to you, we also have to finish some business in Ephesus on Chloe's behalf.'

'You are welcome, Achaicus,' cried Paul. 'You are living proof that the Holy Spirit is still working in the church at Corinth – praise God for that!'

He clapped his hands to summon a servant with refreshment for his friends, and settled them all down on the stone benches encircling a small pool in the centre of the courtyard. Then he seated himself, and faced them squarely.

'Now, let us talk. I want to know all about what is happening in Corinth. I have read the letter you brought, and I'm happy about the *good* news in it. But I have also heard, from other sources, that all is not as it should be. Apparently there have been some serious quarrels among the elders. So, tell me the truth. How are things really?'

Fortunatus and Achaicus both looked at Stephanas who was obviously the designated spokesman of the group. But Stephanas did not respond at first and when he did, it was with some reluctance.

'Well ... yes ... I have to admit there have been some differences. But nothing too serious.'

Paul was not to be put off. 'What kind of differences? Differences over the gospel?'

Again Stephanas hesitated: 'Yes ... there are some problems there. But big arguments are usually about the leadership of the church.'

'Leadership? The elders have all been appointed through the laying on of hands. Aren't they in charge?'

'They ... are divided among themselves.'

'You mean, they are quarrelling over which one should be "top dog"?'

'No ... it goes deeper than that. They are dividing into factions, each claiming that they alone are the true followers of the Way and that everyone else has got it wrong. Wrangling over you and Apollos and Peter. Arguing over which of you is the true apostle of God. I say that *you* are the one we should follow – after all, you planted the church and I certainly believe God has anointed your ministry. A number of the older members – those who were there since the beginning – agree with me. But there is another group who say that Apollos is much the better preacher. They love his expositions of the scriptures and consider his interpretation of them to be intellectually superior. They feel he is the one to bring in new people, especially the Greeks.'

Paul had risen to his feet and was pacing about the courtyard.

'That's absurd,' he said. 'Apollos and I are of one mind and always have been. I've never differed from him about the gospel. God has given special gifts to each of us, and we are brothers in his service. I can't believe the elders are behaving like this.'

He came to an abrupt halt in front of Stephanas. In spite of his short stature he seemed to tower over him, and the fierce glint in his eye made Stephanas more than a little nervous. He avoided Paul's glare.

'Just how many of these factions are there?'

'Er ... Well ... Another group, mostly people who came to us from the synagogue, say that both you and Apollos have departed from the true faith, particularly as it is taught in the Jewish scriptures. They claim to be followers of Peter, who is undoubtedly an apostle. They say we should continue to observe the rules they followed in the synagogue.

'And there's yet another group – a smaller one – who call themselves "the Christ party". They claim that James has the backing of the church in Jerusalem, and just as Jesus and James were not married, so neither should we be. They are in contact with the Essene community who live in the Dead Sea wilderness. Marriage is not allowed among the Essenes, because they don't believe that fleshly desires should be indulged.'

Paul's voice shook with emotion: 'This is monstrous! Those elders are contradicting all I ever taught them. In Christ we are all one – Jews and Greeks, men and women, slaves and freemen. And those of us called to be apostles are servants of Jesus, not rivals and leaders of factions. They're no better than the half-baked philosophers and would-be hucksters one finds ranting down in the Forum, all scrambling to outdo each other. What a shambles! Tell me, Fortunatus, is this how you see what is happening?'

'I'm afraid it is,' replied Fortunatus. 'What is worse, the trouble has even affected the way we take part in the Breaking of the Bread.'

'Quarrelling? At the Lord's Supper?'

'It's not that they are quarrelling so much as behaving selfishly. In the early days the church was mostly made up of very ordinary people – not many well-to-do or influential folk – including a good number of slaves. We all shared together, as you taught us. But then a number of wealthy people joined us and things changed. We used to share our food with each other. Now the rich folk bring their rich food, and plenty of it. They sit in little cliques together, and eat and drink well while the poorer members look on, hungry and half-starved. Then they all have the Breaking of Bread and pretend to be one big happy family. It's just like that story our Lord told – Lazarus starves at the gate while Dives feasts in his mansion. To make it worse, some of them drink too much wine and can hardly hold the cup of blessing steady when they take it.'

'Stop!' cried Paul. 'Say no more! I can hardly bear to listen. This is dreadful and will surely call down judgement upon them.'

There was a tense, unhappy silence, finally interrupted by the apostle.

'I suspect you have still not told me everything. Give me the complete dismal picture. What about those problems in the meetings which they mentioned in their letter?'

Stephanas sighed. 'The fact is they get quite disorderly. Several people speak at once, some in unknown languages and some uttering what they call "prophecies", though there is no one to interpret what they are saying. They all try to outdo each other and get the attention of the others, sometimes actually contradicting each other in the process. Once or twice strangers have come in, seen the confusion and hurried out again, saying we are all mad! The women join in, and the whole thing becomes meaningless and worthless.'

'Anything else?'

'There is one more thing.' Stephanas voice was husky with trepidation. 'It concerns Paphros, the wine merchant.'

'I remember him. Didn't his mother die while I was there? And, just before I left, his father was planning to marry again, I think.'

'That's right, he did. Just after you left. But it wasn't a good marriage. The age gap between them was pretty wide, and Paphros's father became very demanding and consumed with jealousy every time his young wife even looked at another man. Finally, she could stand it no longer and ran away from him.'

'Have they divorced?'

'No, it's worse than that! She has gone and fallen in love with Paphros, and now they're living together openly as man and wife.'

'What?! Have they no sense of shame? I hope the church has expelled them!'

'Well, no, it hasn't. Paphros still comes to the meetings, though Julia doesn't. The elders say that they are only demonstrating their freedom in Christ. Some of those outside the church have heard about it and are shocked. They say that they would never sanction such goings on.'

Paul returned to pacing the courtyard as he tried to take in the news. 'They didn't mention this at all in their letter. Either they thought I wouldn't want to know or, worse, they don't think it a serious issue "worth causing an upset over". But you're one of the elders, Stephanas. How could you allow this?'

'I've done my best to make the truth plain,' said the unhappy Stephanas, 'but I'm only one against seven. The others say I'm only acting as your stooge, trying to shore up your waning influence. They say things have changed since you were there, and we should move with the times, keep up with the new ways of thinking.'

Paul didn't speak for a long time. His face lost its anger and instead became rather sad. 'This alters everything. I'll have to postpone my visit to Corinth – I fear what I would say to them if I were to go feeling as I do. The church must be given time to think through what they are doing, to repent and make some profound changes. I must get a message to Timothy asking him not to go there yet, either. I'll write a reply to their letter and Titus will take it for me. He can report back to me about what happens after that.

'But first, to prayer. The enemy has gained more than a foothold in Corinth, and I must try to understand the mind of God while I write my reply. The care of all the churches, on top of the hard time we are having here at Ephesus – these are burdens I must give over to the Lord. And you all must join with me in the spiritual battle.'

The lamps burned very late that evening.

First thing in the morning, Gaius armed himself with writing materials and made ready for a long, hard day.

THE RETORT COURTEOUS

1 Corinthians 1:1–9

Before Paul got to work on his reply, he must have spent some time considering how he should begin. He was deeply hurt and shocked by what he had heard – it would have been easy to write an angry and punitive response, denouncing the elders for their failure to lead and for tolerating gross error, thundering warnings of judgement against them. But he does not. As in the majority of his letters to the churches he established, he begins by dwelling on the positive, thanking God for the believers and encouraging them (1 Cor 1:4–9).

In view of what follows, this is generous of Paul to say the least: there is so much to rebuke and correct. But Paul is no insurance salesman 'buttering up' his client before making a sales pitch. He deliberately avoids using any 'tricks of the trade' (2:1). Instead he emphasises that it is the grace and mercy *of God* which has been responsible for the planting of churches in the towns and cities of the Roman empire, and 'his grace given you in Christ Jesus' (1:4) which has drawn citizens of Corinth away from licentiousness and idolatry onto the firm ground of 'Jesus Christ and him crucified' (2:2).

Those of us who come to faith suddenly or when we are relatively mature may consciously recognise this separation from our former way of life and from the life of the world around us, and the process may cause us a great deal of tension and heartache. Those who have been brought up in Christian families, who have grown up in the faith, may find the distinction more blurred. But in both cases it is worth holding onto this amazing truth – it was God's grace and mercy that drew us to Christ in the first place: 'We love because he first loved us' (1 John 4:19). God's grace and mercy established a church in your neighbourhood and in the nation in which you are living. In spite of the church's imperfections, in spite of your own, thank God for his gift of faith – your own and that of other Christians.

Paul does make some tactful references to the church's shortcomings as he gently reminds them of his apostolic status, which some of them were questioning (1 Cor 1:1), and emphasises the call to 'be holy' (v 2). But, other than that, he is generally affirming. In spite of the paganism permeating their culture and the dark forces arrayed against them, God has saved them and is offering them 'grace and peace' – priceless gifts in the turbulent world of the Roman empire, and in our own today.

We may be tempted to despair as we pray for our fellow-citizens, who are often trivialised, and sometimes brutalised, by the negative influences that exist in our culture. We may ask, 'Who then can be saved?' Jesus' answer to this question still stands: 'with God all things are possible' (Matt 19:26). And there were Christians in Corinth to prove it.

The honoured name

The inspired apostle does not waste words: he writes compact, high-density truth. So when he gives Jesus his full title – Jesus Christ our Lord – five times in nine verses (1 Cor 1:1–9), we should pause to consider why, particularly in view of the often casual way the name 'Jesus' is used today (not just as a secular swear word). Jesus may become so familiar to Christians that we are in danger of losing any sense of his glorious significance and thus fail to take hold of the blessing he is capable of bringing us. The people in Jesus' home town fell into this trap (Mark 6:1–6). They were impressed by his wise teaching and had heard all about his miracles: but they knew his family; they had seen him grow up; he was only the carpenter who had worked on the building sites in and around Nazareth. So they missed their day of salvation and Jesus 'could not do many miracles there, except lay his hands on a few sick people and heal them'.

Obviously, in focusing on Jesus' full title Paul is emphasising 'our Lord' as against the many 'lords' – the gods and goddesses – that abounded in Corinth (1 Cor 8:5). But '*our* Lord Jesus' would have sufficed for that. Perhaps Paul is delivering a hint to the Corinthian church – and to us? Jesus' full title gives emphasis to his saving power, his special authority as God's Son and the pre-eminence he should have in our lives. If we fail to see his presence in the world around us, our faith becomes little more than a moral code for living or just another philosophical perspective on life. This attitude was becoming apparent in Corinth where factions were forming around those whose basis for faith was intellectual (the 'Apollos party') and those who saw things mainly in terms of rules (the 'Peter party'). But Jesus didn't come to found another 'belief system'. His message focuses on a relationship – the relationship between God and ourselves. To develop a relationship with someone means that we acknowledge them and their importance to us, and share our lives with them. So, in our prayer and our worship, by acknowledging him in all that we do, we develop our relationship with Jesus and, through him, with God.

Paul's graciousness is shown in the gentle way in which he refers to those things that were at the root of so much of the trouble in Corinth – 'speaking', 'knowledge' and the 'spiritual gifts' (1:5, 7). For the moment he is merely content to note that these have been given to the church by God. Later, he will deal severely with the way the Corinthians have abused these gifts. We should also remember that though we may view with dismay those who abuse God's gifts, we would be as much in the wrong if we allowed their abuse to cause us to reject them altogether. God has given the spiritual gifts for *our* benefit, to build his church into a strong community of faith.

Another gentle hint must surely be lurking in Paul's reference to Christ's return (v 7) – a reminder for them and for us that judgement will be a feature of his coming, a judgement that will reveal self-centred living for the tawdry thing it is. The word Paul uses to describe the Second Coming is significant. It is the Greek word from which we get our 'apocalypse', and its core meaning is 'unveiling' or 'revealing' – 'for we shall see him as he is' (1 John 3:2). This is an aspect of Christ's return that we can put alongside the more common view that his coming again will be to 'judge the living and the dead'. Certainly there will be judgement and a solemn final reckoning; but there will also be overwhelming wonder at the sight of our glorious Lord and Saviour. And, even more amazing, 'we shall be like him' (1 John 3:2). When Jesus comes again, the imperfect church – the people of God with all their flaws and failures – will finally become the sanctified bride of Christ, presented to him 'without blemish and free from accusation' (Col 1:22).

For reflection

- Paul describes believers as 'sanctified' (already made holy) and 'called to be holy' (1 Cor 1:2). How can we be 'made holy (past tense) yet 'called to be holy' (present tense) at the same time? Is Paul contradicting himself, or do you think there is a way that the two can be reconciled?

- Paul describes believers as those who 'call on the name of our Lord Jesus Christ'. Can you 'unpack' this phrase and say what it actually means?

QUARRELSOME LEADERS AND IMMATURE FOLLOWERS

1 Corinthians 1:10–17

Throughout Paul's letter we are made aware of the dangerous effects that cultural practices within Corinthian life were having on the church.

> The turbulence and spirit of faction, the fundamental scepticism, the deplorable relapses, the undue tolerance towards sins of impurity, the intellectual arrogance and philosophical posing, and the very abuse of the gifts of the Spirit for self-display, which seem to have marred the Christian community, were reflections of the life of the restless Greek city itself.
>
> (E M Blaiklock)

This spirit of restlessness remains with us still. There is as much faction and fighting in the world as ever there was. In the West in particular, deep suspicion of the old systems and ideologies have prompted their wholesale deconstruction, yet nothing has been put in their place and there is no common morality that we can all appeal to, except perhaps the motto 'live and let live'. Faced with environmental disaster and seemingly intractable human problems, we are in danger of lapsing into apathy and a feeling of helplessness. We feel we ought to know all the answers, but we make so little impression on the world's troubles. In despair we may seek escape from insecurity and boredom – in drugs, in the ever-expanding entertainment industry, in the world of virtual reality. And, being part of our world, the church is also affected. Christians will always have to deal with the dilemma of being in the world but not of it. We are born into our culture and are brought up in its values – we cannot escape its shaping and moulding us, our attitudes and ways of doing things. While there are good things in the world we live in, it needs real spiritual maturity to know what to make of them.

One of the cultural traits of Corinthian life that was carried over into the church was a tendency to form factions and exalt religious leaders to special, semi-divine status. So splinter groups emerged, each attaching itself to a particular Christian luminary and claiming that their adopted hero most fully embodied their particular doctrinal hobby-horse or philosophical stance. It is difficult to blame Paul, Peter and Apollos for this. The existence of these factions showed that the church community was immature and childish in their faith, and found a dubious satisfaction in the quarrels and backbiting that were going on. By attaching themselves to these 'big names' in the church, the factional leaders were trying to bathe themselves in a kind of reflected glory. They probably didn't anticipate that the men they singled out for such attention would be horrified to find themselves treated in this way.

This practice of rallying round charismatic leaders is one that persists in the church. In the past whole denominations have formed around men who challenged – often with good reason – practices and teaching that had developed in the church which ran contrary to the message of the gospel. But these denominational divisions can be used to 'pigeon-hole' other Christians and put distance between 'us' and 'them'. While the church is certainly in constant need of rebuke and renewal (*semper reformanda*), is it right that this should lead so inevitably to division? Paul seems to imply that it is not, and the fact that division nearly always does occur points to our own immaturity as churches in handling diversity and accepting criticism, in recognising error and being willing to change. Paul's message to the Corinthians is blunt – 'Stop being childish!' (1 Cor 3:1).

'Is Christ divided? Was Paul crucified for you?...' (1:13–17): in view of what God has done, it is ironic that we have come to accept the existence of denominations. We employ such titles as 'Baptist', 'Methodist' and 'Anglican' that assert territorial, institutional or even spiritual distinctives. The four parties named here seem to have a way of turning up throughout church history: the 'Paul' party, followers of their solid, unspectacular, doctrine-oriented founder; the 'Apollos' party, preferring the gifted orator with his impressive Bible expositions (Acts 18:24–28); the Peter party, traditionalists with legalistic emphasis; and the 'Christ' party, claiming to be holier than everyone else and thus nearer the Lord, but in fact merely adding their quota to the growing division.

If this sounds familiar to you, reflect on Paul's plea: 'I appeal to you, brothers, in the name of our Lord Jesus Christ, that all of you agree with one another so that there may be no divisions among you and that you may be perfectly united in mind and thought' (1 Cor 1:10).

Divisions in the church: a tragedy

In many ways, the worst thing about divisions in the church is that they contradict the gospel on which it was founded. Since all its members are helpless sinners who have been forgiven by the grace of God through Christ's death on the cross, they should demonstrate this dependence on Christ by showing common allegiance to him. So Paul moves naturally on to the theme that dominates his entire response – the cross (v 17), the touchstone of Christian belief and the controlling principle of Christian behaviour. As he puts it vividly elsewhere (Gal 2:20), 'I have been crucified with Christ.' In every relationship and in all circumstances of life, we must be controlled by that pattern of sacrificial love and active concern for others which Jesus demonstrated at Calvary.

In terms of verse 17 – that we are sent to preach the gospel 'not with words of human wisdom, lest the cross of

Christ be emptied of its power' – the labels we attach to ourselves ought to be marginal at best. Divisions are a scandal because they are the outcome of human ways of thinking. Our ability to receive and understand the full meaning of the cross does not depend on intellectual capacity but, in part, on spiritual maturity (1 Cor 3:1–4). Are we open enough to the working of the Holy Spirit, to allow him to change us and our attitude to others so that we can see them, in spite of any differences, as those whom Christ also died to save? Are we willing to let this perspective strengthen our faith, so that we can entrust those differences to Christ and instead seek to find common ground between us and our fellow Christians? This process may be extremely painful and indeed it may sometimes feel that we really have 'died to self'. But only if we have received the Holy Spirit are we able to take this on board and live the cross-like life.

For reflection

- Accepting the fact that there were differences between the ministries of Paul, Apollos and Peter, was it inevitable that the members of the church at Corinth would be divided in their loyalties?

  How do you think your own church might anticipate and handle differences so that splinter groups or mass walk-outs are avoided? When divisions do occur, who is responsible – the leaders or the members of the church?

  Is there ever a time when a church has no choice but to split up?

- 'Words of human wisdom' can 'empty the cross of its power' (1 Cor 1:17). Can you think of any examples, from your own experience, of how this might happen?

BACK TO BASICS: THE CROSS
WHERE WEAKNESS IS STRENGTH

1 Corinthians 1:18 – 2:5

Paul has so much to say and so many points to make that the words and ideas tumble out. Gone is the ordered structure of the letter to Rome, written at Corinth, with its systematic theological framework. He is writing more from the heart than from the head, inspired by the same Spirit who uses all our gifts and abilities (and moods) to achieve his ends. Only the Spirit, who is the source of all unity (Eph 4:3), is able to counteract the spirit of faction that is causing so much trouble, so Paul develops his argument against divisions in the church by contrasting the wisdom that comes from human sources and that which comes from the Spirit.

No sooner does he mention the gospel (1 Cor 1:17) than he is at the point of this gospel's central truth, and his central theme – the cross of Christ. And so we move at once into a statement that forms the focal point of Paul's life and work – 'the message of the cross is foolishness to those who are perishing, but to us who are being saved it is the power of God' (v 18); in particular – and very important in prestige-seeking Corinth – the wonder of the fact that a symbol of disgrace and defeat should be the instrument of new life and salvation for the world. Remember, Paul did not just preach at people; he 'argued' ('reasoned', NIV) with doubters, (Acts 18:4). No doubt he heard the Christian gospel dismissed by the Greek intelligentsia in Corinth as 'barbaric', 'crude', offensive', 'naive', simplistic' and so on. And the more practical Jews, with their way of judging by results, found it offensive, 'a stumbling block', to believe in one whose death was, in human terms, a demonstration of impotence. No doubt some of the more cultured members of the church were apt to be embarrassed when challenged by their sophisticated neighbours about a religion that was centred on a condemned criminal.

These ways of thinking persist. Many learned, intellectually gifted people label the gospel message as simply foolish, only for the naive inadequate who need some sort of psychological crutch. Others dismiss it outright: there is no God – we are all here through a series of random processes which had no originator – so there is no such thing as sin and redemption, and we have no need of a redeemer. More practically minded critics assert that the continuing existence of sin and suffering on the earth has proved that Christianity has failed.

Human beings have a tendency to think that their own way of understanding things is the right one, but God puts paid to this notion (1 Cor 1:20–25). Paul is uncompromising. Intellectual philosophy, with all its glossy brilliance, and shrewd pragmatism cannot help those who are hungry to know the one true and living God. We should not unthinkingly accept the secular viewpoint as the only way to understand life. While science and philosophy will help us to go some way towards understanding God's creation and aspects of his character, they cannot help us develop a relationship with him through Christ, which is the principal way that we come to know him (v 24).

The church: a community without distinctions

The Countess of Huntingdon, deeply involved in the eighteenth century revival in Britain, said that she thanked God for the 'm' in 'many' (v 26). However, at Corinth membership of the church was at first mainly drawn from the poorer and socially marginalised section of the community – people who didn't count for anything. As it had been when Jesus was on earth, it was the 'common people' who were the first to respond to the gospel message. There were 'not many' of the influential, 'not many' of noble birth. But later, more educated wealthy people did join the church, and this led to particularly unfortunate divisions (11:18–22). Diversity can make for a bumpy journey together in the Christian faith.

But Paul does not see this as a negative factor, as we tend to. For him it is further proof that the church exists because of what *God* has done. A movement which attracts only the wealthy and influential in society can attract members who want to join for all the wrong reasons, hoping to climb the ladder of worldly success or respectability. The only authentic motive for joining the church is a deep hunger for the living God and a profound need to be right with him. God has to take the initiative and draw men, women and children, by his Spirit, to himself (1:27). An authentic church is one which totally depends on God and looks to the Holy Spirit as the primary force in its development as a community. When we judge a church's spiritual temperature purely in terms of numbers, or how jazzed up the worship seems to be, or the amount of evangelistic programmes it runs, we are missing the point and may be guilty of being unfair or simply wrong. A small church struggling to keep the gospel alive in a spiritually 'dark' neighbourhood is serving God just as surely as a large church with lots of programmes and dynamic services. The Scottish preacher who 'only' led one young lad to the Lord did as much for the kingdom as some of his more 'successful' colleagues – that lad was David Livingstone, who later went on to take the gospel to Africa.

A big problem for the church in the West is its tendency to be so strongly middle-class that people from other social backgrounds perceive themselves as neither belonging nor of being wanted. Those who do join soon begin to feel uncomfortable for fear that they must recast themselves in a new mould so that they can fit in. It is understandable that a group of people will attract others who are like-minded, and sometimes this is viewed as a positive method for church growth: the more people a church can attract the better, and if it can only do this by drawing one particular type of person, then so be it – at least more people are coming. However, this leads to churches full of Christians who never learn how to deal with differences because they have never had the experience of relating to those with other opinions and attitudes. The outcome is a 'monochrome' church – dull, unchallenging and unadventurous – which outsiders see as a clique of people uninterested in their concerns and with nothing to offer them. Paul's remedy for clashes in personality or differences in social status within the church at Corinth is not to keep everybody happy by letting them form single-interest groups. He simply says they should learn to get on with each other: this is part of their Christian witness and the primary means of their becoming mature in faith. The rest of his letter outlines how they could set about doing this.

The four qualities listed in verse 30 should be read as one all-inclusive quality, wisdom, with three component parts – righteousness, holiness and redemption (NIV). Paul compares the wisdom of God with that wisdom of which the sophisticated Corinthians are boasting – their scheme of philosophy that gives them a 'complete' world-view. 'However,' he says, 'we have a world-view too. It is made up of three ingredients very different from your philosophical speculations – righteousness, sanctification and redemption.' None of these aspects featured in the Corinthian scheme. Righteousness was not a high priority for the citizens of Corinth: opportunities to live the good life lay all around them and those who could did and those who couldn't looked on in envy. Sanctification was not a prominent consideration either: the devotees of the various temples tried to appease their gods and goddesses, hoping that in doing so they would gain entry to the good life; but these attempts at appeasement had little to do with the character of the worshipper. Redemption hardly featured at all, except perhaps as a business transaction to buy someone out of slavery.

Righteousness, sanctification and redemption are alien concepts in our own culture. Like the Corinthians we do what is necessary to achieve wealth and status, and those who succeed are envied and given pre-eminence. Self-improvement is perceived as coming through our own efforts, more to do with academic success (or being 'smart') and looking good than it has to do with being 'made holy'. And as for redemption – no-one else can save you; you save yourself.

But righteousness is not simply moral uprightness; rather it is the condition of a believer knowing he is accepted as righteous by God himself, and knowing this acceptance is only possible because Christ's righteousness is credited to the believer as a result of his death on the cross. Sanctification – being made holy – is only possible through the action of the Holy Spirit. Redemption – being brought back into a right relationship with God – is only possible because Christ took our punishment on the cross. These three ingredients are therefore centred on the cross and add up to true wisdom from God.

How an apostle sets about his task

'When I came to you, brothers, I did not come with eloquence or superior wisdom as I proclaimed to you the testimony about God.'

1 Corinthians 2:1–5 is a uniquely important self-exposure of Paul the apostle at work. On the face of it, his was the 'mission impossible' – a travelling Jewish preacher confronting a great city with a message that gave primacy to a crucified criminal. Earning his own living and accompanied by a couple of Jewish refugees from a pogrom in Rome (Acts 18:2–3), Paul made things more difficult for himself at Corinth by deliberately refusing to win a hearing by clever techniques (1 Cor 2:4–5). Corinthians were connoisseurs of rhetoric; Paul renounced it. Corinthians loved playing with ideas; Paul preached straightforward truth. This decision to run counter to what was expected

from him was not incidental. The things he refused to do might have attracted attention and won him approval; but they might also have diverted his hearers from the most important part of his message – 'Jesus Christ and him crucified' (v 2). This phrase is worth dwelling on because it sums up those two aspects of the gospel that we have looked at already.

First, it makes clear that the Christian gospel is about a *person*, not a system of doctrine or a rule of living, important as these may be. Relating to Jesus Christ as a person is the essential experience of the Christian. As he said to the first disciples, 'Follow *me*.'

Second, 'Jesus Christ and him crucified' centres on an event that is firmly rooted and grounded in history. Christianity is not a philosophy or the product of great human intellect: it happened in a place at a particular time. And this event was both tragic and glorious, demanding suffering and sacrifice, but becoming the source of hope and new life for those who confess their unworthiness and put their trust in what Jesus achieved in that time and place.

For reflection

- Can you think of any real-life examples of how God has 'made foolish the wisdom of the world', and of how he has chosen 'the weak things of the world to shame the strong' (1 Cor 1:18–29)?

- 'When I came to you, brothers, I did not come with eloquence or superior wisdom as I proclaimed to you the testimony about God' (1 Cor 2:1).

  How far should this be taken as a guideline for preaching? Does it mean that evangelists and preachers should not say *anything* that would make them and their message attractive to unbelievers? What about jokes from the pulpit?!

GOD'S FOOLISH WISDOM

1 Corinthians 2:6 – 3:4

There is always pressure on Christians to adjust their faith so that it fits in with the current philosophies of the day, and this is what seemed to have been happening in Corinth. But Paul's reply is that it is God's intention finally to destroy these philosophies (1 Cor 1:19)!

In a sense, they destroy each other as successive generations develop new ways of thinking and move on from what has come before. One school of thought after another comes into being and is overthrown or abandoned in its turn. In recent times we have seen such systems as the enlightenment, existentialism and logical positivism come and go, and now post-modernist thinking takes centre stage. It is amazing evidence of the liveliness of God's word that his answer to all these alternatives remains the positive truth of the gospel.

There exists a style of debate which tries to beat an opponent by exaggerating or caricaturing his arguments. So some at Corinth might have argued that, because Paul rejected philosophical ideas and intellectual forms of debate (2:4–5), there was no wisdom to be had in the Christian faith and thus its teaching was rendered worthless. 'Not so,' counters the apostle. 'We have wisdom all right – but it is God's wisdom.' No matter how impressive their scholarly or religious qualifications, no matter how high they were in their political or social standing, those who crucified Christ demonstrated their ignorance (v 8) by refusing to take account of this godly wisdom.

God's wisdom stands over and above human wisdom

and is not easily understood by it (1:21). What seems logical and even sensible to us may, from God's perspective, be folly. Christians may struggle with this knowledge as we try to discern the right way forward in situations where there are no clear guidelines to follow. It is a cause for thanksgiving that God is often able to work through human systems and beliefs in order to bring his wisdom into being (eg Dan 1:17–20; 2:14–23).

The 'go-between' God

'Oracles' – messages of 'wisdom' claiming to come from one or other of the pagan deities – were a feature of religion in the temples of Corinth. The whole process lent itself to fraud and quackery. Paul points to an altogether different source of wisdom: the Holy Spirit is mentioned seven times in close succession (1 Cor 2:10–14). This is surely significant. John Calvin emphasised the need for the scriptures to be 'illuminated' by the Spirit: if they are not, they are mere dead letter. In this passage, see how Paul speaks of the Holy Spirit as the 'go-between' God, the most reliable guide we have (John 16:13). The Spirit searches 'the deep things of God' and then instils what he finds in the believer who has spiritual discernment (1 Cor 1:14). This may be the least spectacular but most important aspect of the Spirit's ministry to us. Without his help we can easily distort scripture to our own destruction, as many do (2 Peter 3:16).

The same Spirit acts as a 'go-between' at the human level. When we share together in the things of God, both those doing the speaking and those doing the listening need to be led by the Spirit. We sometimes forget this whenever we evangelise or try to explain our faith and think only in terms of the speaker having to break down the listener's resistance. This is not how God works, and the assumption behind all our witness should be that sharing the truths of the gospel is a process which must be prepared for by prayer and carried out in absolute dependence on the Spirit.

Paul introduces us to three types of people:

- 'the man without the Spirit', ie the non-believer;
- 'the spiritual man', ie the true believer (1 Cor 2:14–15);
- the 'men of flesh' (misleadingly translated 'worldly' in the NIV, 3:1, 3), ie believers who have been baptised by the Spirit (12:13) but who are certainly not living by the Spirit (Rom 8:13–14).

The Corinthians put themselves into this last category partly because of their spiritual immaturity (1 Cor 3:1). These 'fleshly' Christians continue to allow their old way of life to dominate: like those in Luke 9:62 who kept looking back, old habits and old ties remain firmly established and they are unable to move on in their faith. They have not given of their best to the work of God's kingdom, and what they have given won't last, because they have not developed their spiritual skills enough so as to contribute anything of long-lasting value. Like those who escape from a burning house and have nothing left but the clothes they stand up in, their salvation remains intact through God's grace, but they are stripped of the reward they might have received from him (1 Cor 3:15). They are lukewarm like the Laodiceans (Rev 3:16) who were neither cold nor hot' and who were therefore unpalatable ('I am about to spit you out of my mouth'). These 'fleshly' Christians may regard themselves as shrewd and worldly wise, but they are spiritually stunted.

Spiritual 'Peter Pans'

Paul makes a small but very significant change in the word he uses for 'fleshly' ('worldly') (1 Cor 3:1, 3). When he started at Corinth, he had preached and taught the basics of the gospel (15:1–2), and there was nothing wrong then in the new converts' being 'fleshly' or immature in the early days of their Christian experience. This was only to be expected, in the same way that a baby is a weak and dependent creature. But the word Paul uses in verse 3 refers to the Corinthians' continuing attitude, their persistent babyishness. They were like grown-ups still demanding a four-hourly bottle of milk.

This may seem, on the face of it, to be a harsh judgement. But, says Paul, 'the facts give you away. Your party labels, your tribal disputes, prove that you haven't grown up. You may talk learnedly about Pauline doctrine and Petrine ecclesiology and Apollonian exegesis, but the very fact that you think and speak in those terms proves your puerility.' Moreover, the Corinthian Christians give themselves away not by some gross or blatant sin but by their everyday, individual behaviour – 'jealousy and quarrelling' – and projecting their own differences of opinion onto their unwitting, unwilling leaders. There was, in fact, no quarrel between Paul and Apollos: they are never seen at variance in the New Testament. There may have been a more serious problem with the group forming around Peter ('Cephas', 1:12) who may have been pressing for a more legalistic version of Christianity; but Paul fought this pressure uncompromisingly because it undermined the central truth of the Christian faith (Gal 3:1–5).

Growing into maturity

How do we define what being 'mature' in faith really means? The Greek word Paul uses (1 Cor 2:6) is often translated 'perfect' in the New Testament. It conveys the idea of being fully developed or grown into adulthood. The Christian life is a process which takes time, which needs nourishment and which must be trained. In our enthusiasm at welcoming new believers into the family of faith, we are apt to forget that these young Christians need this time and training before they can take on major responsibilities within the church – hence Paul's warning to Timothy that a man overseeing a church should not be a recent convert (1 Tim 3:6).

The word Paul uses for 'mature' was in fact also used

by the pagan religions flourishing in Corinth to describe those who had been 'initiated' into the 'mysteries' of that religion. It is perhaps surprising that Paul does not hesitate to employ a word with such associations; but the difference is that while initiation ceremonies in the temples consisted of outward ceremonies and rituals, Christian maturity is a matter of personal growth and transformation by the Spirit in the inner self (2 Cor 3:17–18).

Paul has as yet made no reference to the more spectacular ministries of the Spirit who prompts the mind of the believer – 'his that gentle voice we hear, soft as the breath of even'. Nor is it incidental that twice he clinches a point by quoting from the Old Testament: verse 9 relates back to Isaiah 64:4, and verse 16 to Isaiah 40:13. 'The Spirit breathes upon the word and brings the truth to sight.' The written word of scripture defines the boundaries beyond which we are not to go in speculating about the truth. Whenever we can, we should always use the Bible as a source from which we can draw principles to follow in our lives, praying all the while that the Spirit will help us discern the truth. This does not mean that there is no room for fresh thinking and for making the truth relevant to our ever-changing cultural and intellectual environment. There is plenty of scope for using scripture within the exercise of all the intellectual and spiritual gifts we may possess. But beyond the boundaries of scripture lie swamps of confusion and minefields of heresy. An important safeguard against going astray is to discuss any ideas or doubts we may have within a community of Christians who can check our interpretations. History is full of examples of individualism leading to error.

And finally, we should always come back to the life and character of Jesus, to whom we can look as the supreme example of how we should be light to the people we know and to the culture we live in.

For reflection

- The keyword in this section is 'mature'. How do you define spiritual maturity? The following references may help: Proverbs 16:21–27; Galatians 4:3; Ephesians 4:13; Philippians 3:15; Colossians 1:28; 4:12; 1 Timothy 3:6; Hebrews 6:1.

- What do you think is the 'milk' of the gospel? What is the 'solid food'?

   How do we distinguish between an infantile quarrel in the church and a legitimate difference of judgement on a subject of serious spiritual concern?

PERILS AND PRIVILEGES OF CHRISTIAN LEADERSHIP

1 Corinthians 3:5 – 4:5

By splitting into rival factions, the Corinthian church is threatening to drive a wedge between Paul and Apollos. Paul's answer is not to deny that he and Apollos differ in their teaching but rather to put them both into a category which makes any rivalry absurd. He and Apollos are no more than God's servants, 'field-labourers' on his farm. It is God alone who gives life and who causes it to grow to a full harvest (1 Cor 3:7). Three times in verse 9, the word 'God' is emphasised in the Greek by being put at the beginning of each clause – thus 'God's fellow-workers are we, God's field are you, God's building...'

Paul is pointing to a tragic error in the Corinthian church. By making too much of human leaders and by dividing themselves they are deposing God from his rightful supremacy (v 5). We may smile at the child who points to his own tiny corner of the garden and boasts of the 'flowers which I growed'. But we must give short shrift to the farmer surveying a field in which the wheat stands tall, or the executive closing the book on a completed project, who says proudly, 'All my own work!' At best we are participators in God's overall purpose for ourselves as individuals and for the human race in general. Humility is one of the hall-marks of a Christian. While we must be aware of the dangers of complete self-effacement and low self-esteem and make every effort to affirm one another's talents and qualities, we must also acknowledge that these come from God. We can get satisfaction, however, from the knowledge that we are taking part in his work of bringing his kingdom into the world.

The most impressive building

Verses 10–15 go beyond making a general comment on building the Christian life. The context shows that Paul is referring directly to the church at Corinth. He has laid the foundation – Jesus Christ. There is surely some hint of the troubles the church is experiencing in his observation that 'someone else is building on it' (v 10) – a possible reference perhaps to the 'Peter' faction (1:12)? If this is the case, then the groups of materials mentioned refer specifically to the materials that the church builders are using (3:12): the 'gold' of Christ-centred truth; the 'silver' of the pure gospel of grace; the 'precious stones' of loving mutual service; the 'stubble' of legalism; the 'hay' of superficial emotionalism. Ultimately, on the Day of Judgement, the true value of each will be revealed. Wherever churches are planted and new converts made, we need to remember that these new communities in the faith require solid foundations and strong construction materials in order to weather the storms that will surely rage around them (Matt 7:27).

Corinth was a city of majestic temples, none greater than those dedicated to Apollo or Aphrodite, whose priestesses (sacred prostitutes) did much to corrupt Corinthian life. The true temple of God was not a visible building at all: it was the small company of believers who met together in someone's house (1 Cor 3:16). The marble and gold of the city's pagan temples seemed solid and impressive as if they would last forever: but today they are no more. The church of Jesus Christ bestrides the world: the material with which it is built is more enduring. But note Paul's warning – fostering or tolerating divisions among God's people is like planting a bomb in God's temple, incurring his certain judgement (v 17).

The most dangerous enemy

The most dangerous enemy to the Christian life is named in verse 18 – self-deceit. To be deceived by events is bad;

to be deceived by false teaching is worse; to be deceived by Satan worse still (Rev 13:14; 20:2–3, 10). But in all these instances the source of deceit comes from outside ourselves and, if we will, we can recognise it for what it is.

But *self*-deceit is the most dangerous: it comes from inside and can easily pass by our defences unnoticed. In the Corinthian church there were people who were sincerely propagating wrong ideas – hedonism dressed up as 'freedom in Christ' and legalism disguised as holy living. Paul reiterates that God's wisdom is distinct from ours and finds its ultimate focus in Jesus Christ (1 Cor 3:21–23). Those who contend with others over different opinions of doctrine or over church leadership – that is, who 'boast in men' – are small-minded and mean-spirited. In the light of God's overwhelming mercy and eternal purpose, such squabbling is no more than a sick joke.

Paul accuses the church members of deceiving themselves if they are under the impression that they should be the ones to pass judgement on their leaders (4:1). Church leaders are not our overlords but God's servants, and the only one who can justly, fairly and accurately assess their work – or indeed the work of any Christian, for we are all called to be his servants (1 Pet 4:10) – is God. Those who are quick to pass judgement on others cannot read 'the motives of men's hearts' (1 Cor 4:5), so they are more than likely to get it wrong and to cause much disruption and unhappiness. Paul calls the church to be patient and to refrain from passing judgement. When the Lord returns his judgement will be perfect, for he will 'bring to light what is hidden in darkness and will expose the motives of men's hearts'.

This should discourage us from being overly critical of ourselves and others. We may think that we know just what our spiritual state is and what we have achieved, or have not achieved, as Christians. But it is not our task to make such an assessment. Rather we should get on with the life of serving Christ and leave him to give us praise or censure. This does not mean that there is no room for occasional self-assessment so that we can be more whole-hearted and more effective in our faith. Nor does it mean that other people's assessment of us won't sometimes be accurate! But in the end, we cannot anticipate what the Lord's final judgement on us will be. That we cannot escape! This should make us somewhat watchful over our own concerns and behaviour, and a little more cautious about leaping to conclusions about those of others. Judging is not really our business.

For reflection

- 'What, after all, is Apollos? And what is Paul? Only servants, through whom you came to believe – as the Lord has assigned to each his task. I planted the seed, Apollos watered it, but God made it grow' (1 Cor 3:5–6).

  Using these verses as a guide to your thinking, what do you consider are the most important factors in evangelism and church growth?

- What does Paul mean when he says, 'All things are yours' (1 Cor 3:21)? Is this just inspirational rhetoric, or does it have 'cash value'?

SPIRITUAL ARROGANCE DEFLATED

1 Corinthians 4:6–21

Until this point Paul has been restrained in his response to the scandalous behaviour exhibited by members of the church at Corinth: now he releases the full force of his heartfelt concern for them. As we read what he says and the powerful verbal weaponry he uses – burning sarcasm, direct admonition, reminders of their debt to him and warnings – we need to clear our minds of the sentimentality that so easily clouds our thinking when we ponder the meaning of love within Christian relationships. It is because Paul cares about the church and for its members that he does not spare them. The temptation to be harsh about others behind their backs and mealy-mouthed to their faces is often very strong, yet it can actually be evidence of how little we really think of them.

The Greek word for 'puffed up' (1 Cor 4:6, RSV, rather inadequately rendered 'take pride in' in the NIV) was obviously much in Paul's mind. The word appears in various forms throughout this letter (vs 18–19; 5:2; 8:1) and is a clue to one characteristic of the church that was giving the apostle cause for concern. The very fact that they were forming factions and pitting one leader against the other was evidence of their arrogance. And arrogance – assuming superior knowledge or, even worse, superior spirituality – is a deadly plague. If taken to the extreme, it can lead to shocking abuses. Wherever people give precedence to human systems of thought over and above common humanity, their attitude towards and treatment of other people deteriorates and horrific cruelty is nearly always the result. But Paul's warning is 'Do not go beyond what is written'. Scripture cannot be forced to say more than it does or to justify what is mere human wisdom. Everything that the Corinthians had was given to them by God (4:7). They owed their very souls to his grace, and in this they 'were no different from anyone else'. So there is no room for arrogance. When we think of what we have done and compare it with what God has done for us, human pride is completely overthrown.

In verse 6 Paul tactfully omits mentioning Peter: the relationship between himself and Apollos was so straight-forward and untainted by rivalry that he could include him without being accused of undue criticism. But it would not have been so easy with Peter – there were those at Corinth who would be quick to see a slight where none was intended, and Paul was always sensitive to possible misunderstandings by others (see also 8:9).

Bad theology and bad behaviour

The Stoics, who emphasised self-sufficiency, had a catch-phrase: 'I alone am rich; I alone reign as king'. It was surely not an accident that Paul picks up these boasts and pins them on the Corinthian Christians (4:8). They appear to have fallen into the temptation of anticipating God's unfolding plan, claiming that since they were enjoying his kingdom in its fullness already they had nothing more to learn – they were already children of the perfect kingdom, so they could live as they pleased (6:12). They even appear to think their privileged position is one in which neither Paul nor the other apostles have any part ('You have become kings – and that without us!'). Paul replies with heavy irony: 'If only you were right, and then we, the apostles, could share in your good fortune with you!' The Corinthians are blind to the truth: the fact is they are 'wretched, pitiful, poor, blind, and naked' (Rev 3:17).

In order to bring them back to reality, Paul reminds them what it is like to be an apostle. (He is writing from

Ephesus, where he has had a very hard time indeed, Acts 19:23*ff.*) Those 'at the end of the procession' (1 Cor 4:9) were condemned criminals, doomed to die as victims to wild beasts at the climax of a gladiatorial spectacle. If only the Corinthians were right, says Paul. If Christians were indeed already kings, he and his colleagues would have been spared a great deal of suffering and sacrifice (vs 11–13). His moving description of the hardships they suffer makes nonsense of the claims of exponents of the 'prosperity gospel' who say that Christians have a right to health and wealth now, and can have them if they will only exercise enough faith. Suffering is part of the Christian witness: when we suffer we are sharing in Christ, and when we endure we are evidence of his life-giving power and saving love for the whole world. The way we handle suffering gives expression to the hope we have that one day everything will be different: Christ's kingdom will be complete, and suffering and death will be no more (15:51–55; Rev 21:1–4).This way of suffering is very much a reality for many of our fellow-believers around the world. The least we can do is keep track of what is happening to them, through the news and the reports by organisations like Christian Solidarity International or Open Doors, and remember them regularly in prayer.

Paul established the church in Corinth and, spiritually speaking, its members are his children. As such, he asserts, they should show their family likeness by being 'chips off the old block' (1 Cor 4:15–16) and imitating him. Paul is confident of his apostolic authority and of his position as their 'father in the gospel'; he is equally confident that he lives 'in Christ Jesus' and in line with the gospel teaching (v 17): so he is certain that his is a good example to follow and that he is quite able to demonstrate the power of God's kingdom when he next goes to Corinth (vs 19–21).Verse 20 echoes what he has already stressed (2:1–5). The general principle can be summed up in Calvin's comment: 'for how small an affair is it for any one to have the skill to prate eloquently, while he has nothing but empty tinkling'. The factional arguments and philosophical posturing at Corinth were all so much hot air. There is nothing wonderful about someone being adept at speaking well when it is all just talk. The kingdom of God is demonstrated by its effects and not by words; and evidence of the kingdom's power is seen in the changed lives of human beings, who cannot live in the way they know they should without the power of the Holy Spirit. When Paul came to Corinth, he would see what power the 'puffed up' chatterers really had. All their empty philosophising cannot help people to be full citizens of God's kingdom.

Some students of this letter suggest that Paul is ready to sign off at this point: but then the visitors of Corinth arrive with their alarming report of events, and this leads him to carry on. The other possibility is that 1 Corinthians consists of two letters that were later merged into one. Whatever the case, there appears now to be a definite break as the apostle goes on to deal with specific issues raised by the church.

For reflection

- In 1 Corinthians 4:8–13 Paul seems to experience a rush of intense feeling. Read these verses aloud to yourself, giving them their proper dramatic emphasis and getting the feel of the apostle's urgency and passion.

  What do you think it was in the church at Corinth that sparked off this outburst?

- 'When we are cursed, we bless; when we are persecuted, we endure it; when we are slandered, we answer kindly' (1 Cor 4:12–13).

  Can you draw any comparisons between these verses and Jesus' teaching in Matthew 5:1–12, and Paul's teaching in 1 Corinthians 13?

TAKING SIN SERIOUSLY

1 Corinthians 5:1–13; 6:1–20

Paul's mind is saturated with Old Testament teaching, so it is not surprising that he echoes the Old Testament theme of holiness by separation. He now transfers this theme to the context of the New Testament 'temple' – the Christians at Corinth (1 Cor 2:16) – and calls on them not to fraternise with those among them who are incorrigible, unrepentant sinners (5:11). Note the kinds of sins covered. The NIV follows the RSV in translating the first of these as 'immoral': the precise Greek word means 'fornicator'. But all six types of behaviour listed in verse 10 are immoral, and we should not limit this heavily loaded word to sexual offences only.

The major offender in all this is the church which, in its arrogance, is allowing sin to continue unrebuked (5:2). In some subtle way, the leaders have managed to explain away the offender's sin and were perhaps feeling proud of the superior understanding and the assertion of Christian freedom that prompted them to take this approach. But their complacency is ill-advised. Here surely is the need for drastic action: without it, the church's testimony and the Lord's honour are both compromised. The offender, says Paul, should be put out of the fellowship, and the church should dissociate itself from his behaviour. This excommunication and the ban he places on consorting with sinners (5:11) relate specifically to someone 'who calls himself a brother' – a Christian believer who lives immorally. Paul did not forbid social relationships in general with those outside the church (10:27): indeed this would have been impossible in a city like Corinth. Rather, his hope is that the offending individual will still attain his salvation (5:4): the purpose of the excommunication, and the stern command that he be handed over 'to Satan, so that his sinful nature may be destroyed', is that the man might realise his error and repent (5:5).

It is usually left to individual churches or denominations to decide how they handle sinful behaviour within their midst, and to individual Christians how they behave towards the offender. Some denominations do have ecclesiastical courts to deal with particular offences committed by church leaders and others who come within its jurisdiction. But it is worth bearing in mind that Paul's particular censure was directed more towards the Corinthian church for their complacent attitude to sin than towards the individuals who committed it. And we should also remember that 'a little yeast works through the whole batch of dough' (5:6): the behaviour of individual members of the church does have consequences for the whole community. (Paul develops this idea further in 8:9–13.) Perhaps the reason why the church sometimes seems so weak in matters of morality is because we are not concerned enough about sin within our midst. This does not mean there should be hysteria and an all-out witch-hunt. And we should certainly let Christian love, forgiveness and, most important of all, the Holy Spirit be our guides when we deal with sinful behaviour. We need to distinguish carefully between keeping the law in order to be reconciled to God – the legalism of the Pharisees – and honouring the law as expressing the will of God for humankind. In all this we look to the example of Jesus who never tolerated sin but who was still able to show such love for the sinner that this alone was motivation enough to win many people to repent and to change.

Throughout his letter, Paul does not move far from his and the gospel's central theme – the cross. At the centre of his castigation of the church's attitude to sexual error, he reminds them that 'Christ, our Passover lamb, has been sacrificed' (5:7).The Passover lamb was offered up to mark the escape of Israel from slavery in Egypt and the march to freedom in the promised land; in the same way, the cross of Christ marks the escape from bondage to sin and the beginning of a life of freedom as citizens in God's kingdom. God forgives us for Christ's sake, so we do not have to go on trying to justify ourselves: instead we 'rest' on his finished work (Heb 4:9), and then begin to live the new life (Rom 6:11) in which our bodies are offered to God to be 'instruments of righteousness' (Rom 6:13).

Leave lawyers out of it

Paul's discussion about judgement and how it is exercised within the fellowship leads him now to a brief digression about going to the law. The church in Corinth may well have dismissed as harmless the fact that some of their members were taking each other to court to resolve disputes – 'trivial cases' (1 Cor 6:2) that were probably concerned with property or someone's reputation. To Paul this is a serious betrayal of the principles on which the Christian faith is founded. Those who are born again into the kingdom of God share a common life in the Spirit which transcends all normal human relationships: in such a life, disputes should be handled differently from normal society. The Greeks loved litigation (William Barclay) but among God's people this combative spirit could only foster divisions, arguments, a competitive spirit – the need to win and to be seen to win. To have reached such a low point in their community relationships as to bring another believer to court, to be seen putting each other down in front of unbelievers, was surely a poor witness to the reconciliatory power of the gospel (6:7a). To revert to heathen courts was, in effect, to shame Christ and undermine his example of sacrifice and selfless love. Jesus himself taught and lived differently – 'Turn the other cheek', 'Let him have your cloak as well' (Matt 5:39–40).

We may feel that Paul is very extreme in his rejection of

courts. Human systems of justice reflect divine provi-
dence, keeping alive the sense that we should treat each
other fairly, regulating our behaviour towards others, and
ensuring that the poor and the powerless have some
means of gaining redress in a world which frequently
works against them? Perhaps it would help to bear in
mind that Paul is focusing on the Christian community
and the way we treat other believers. Minor disputes
between Christians should be avoided or settled as quickly
as possible; and if there is a major disagreement, everything possible should be done to resolve the issue before
resorting to legal action. Our attitude should be that we
would rather suffer loss (1 Cor 6:7b) than allow the dis-
pute to rumble on and be made worse in the adversarial
atmosphere of a court room. In fact, there will be times
when we will be unable to obtain justice for wrongs done
to us, and then we will need to trust God to resolve the situation, either in this world or the next: 'Leave room for
God's wrath' (Rom 12:19).

Paul says to the believers, 'You yourselves cheat and do
wrong, and you do this to your brothers' (1 Cor 6:8).
Again he makes one of his rare references to the kingdom
of God. Possibly talking about Roman law – one of the
special 'glories' of the empire – reminds him of the kingdom that is set first to overcome and then to replace all
earthly kingdoms. This kingdom is made up of people
who reflect God's holiness, and Paul goes into a list of the
wide range of sinful behaviours that should have no place
in the lives of its citizens (6:9–10). In referring to homo-
sexuality, he uses two precise Greek works which describe
the active and passive partners in homosexual intercourse:
he is clearly referring to homosexual practices rather than
the homosexual disposition.

'And that is what some of you were' – alongside the
doubtless conscientious and morally upright converts
from the Jewish synagogue were those drawn from the
Gentile population in Corinth. They had all been transformed by a process which could be described in three

ways – 'washed', 'sanctified' and justified' (6:11). Some commentators have seen these as three successive stages in the process of conversion, but it seems better to put them alongside each other as three different but complementary ways of making the same point. Each is in the aorist tense, indicating an action that has been completed but which has ongoing consequences. 'Washing' is a straightforward illustration of the cleansing away of defilement; 'sanctified' (ie 'set apart to be holy') marks the revolution in purpose that follows commitment to a holy God; 'justified' speaks of being accepted as righteous in God's sight through the atoning work of Jesus Christ crucified. Each marks a triumph of the gospel over the darkness and corruption of worldly life without Christ. Thus Paul is urging the believers to live up to their new calling, to be transformed in their thinking and behaviour towards each other. In the light of such a transformation, court cases are out of the question.

Taking sexuality seriously

Paul now returns to his theme of immorality. The three quotations (6:12–13) were almost certainly made by the group in the church which were encouraging uninhibited indulgence of bodily appetites on the premise that, for the Christian, the body was a temporary home which would eventually decay, and that what mattered was the 'spirituality' of the believer. They were right to apply this principle to matters like food and drink (Rom 14:17), but wrong to extend it to sexual behaviour. There *are* moral issues related to eating and drinking, and it is recognised that the eating disorders so widespread today (tending to affect women more than men) have as much to with an individual's view of herself and her body, including her sexuality, as with her attitude to food. But moral issues relating to sexual intercourse are broader in their influence. They affect the whole lives of two people physically, emotionally and spiritually, for better or for worse.

Paul is no legalist and he insists on his freedom in Christ; but it is freedom from having to obey the law in order to meet God's demands, not licence to indulge bodily appetites without restraint. He himself speaks later of disciplining his body and keeping it under his control (1 Cor 9:27). The things that we think we choose to indulge in all too often become our taskmasters (6:12), and love-making very easily swamps our consciences with its powerful sensual and emotional appeal.

Sex is not merely a fleshly, animal relationship. Not only is it the means whereby men and women can have a direct part in God's creative purpose, it is also sacramental in that it is intended to be the outward and visible expression of the deepest, most significant human relationship – a pledge of a unique and mutual commitment of man and woman to each other. This is made clear by the way Paul placed it in the context of a believer's relationship with the Lord (6:17). Just as in taking the bread and wine Christians enact an intimate, unique and exclusive relationship with Christ, so in sexual intercourse they enact a special intimacy with their spouse.

Therefore, to behave promiscuously is a kind of sacrilege against the marriage vows. Here Paul is not speaking primarily of extramarital sex but of sex with a prostitute which debases the whole sexual relationship into a sordid transaction providing physical relief and no more (6:16). Such a corruption of God's very special gift of human sexuality is an insult to our Maker. Even the most libertarian Corinthian would have thought twice about going from the Lord's Supper to take part in a ritual meal in the temple of Aphrodite – it would have been unthinkable. So should fornication be for the believer. (Again note that throughout this passage Paul used the precise word for 'fornication'. The RSV and NIV use 'immorality' and 'sexual immorality', which confuses the issue since all sins are 'immoral', not just sexual ones.)

Again, at the core of Paul's appeal for right living is Christ's sacrificial death. We were 'bought at a price'

(6:20) – both the *fact* of the cross and its *meaning* are stressed, and these two aspects should never be divorced. The analogy of purchasing is an important way of understanding our redemption. A purchase is a purposive act with a precise objective. In the same way, Jesus' death was not simply the ultimate gesture of self-sacrificing love; it was a deliberately planned transaction, a price paid for a specific objective – our redemption from sin. 'Christ died for our sins according to the Scriptures' (15:3) – scriptures like Isaiah 53:5, 'he was pierced for our transgressions, he was crushed for our iniquities; the punishment that brought us peace was upon him, and by his wounds we are healed'.

'Do you not know that your body is a temple of the Holy Spirit, who is in you, whom you have received from God?' (1 Cor 6:19). With this tremendous assertion, Paul echoes Jesus' revolutionary statement to the Samaritan woman (John 4:21–24). A temple is a place set apart for worship, for reflection, for encounter with God. The great temple at Jerusalem, Aphrodite's impressive temple at Corinth, the many magnificent gold and marble edifices that soared over the cities of the Roman Empire – all are marginalised by this devastatingly radical principle. 'Don't you know that you yourselves are God's temple and that God's Spirit lives in you?' (1 Cor 3:16, which Paul is addressing to the whole community). These verses take the centre of gravity of worship away from impressive buildings and locate it in the hearts of true believers. Worship, honouring God, proclaiming his truth – when the Christian does all these, he or she is expressing the fact that God's law is not inscribed on jealously guarded tablets of stone but writ large in the heart (Jer 31:33) and lived out in the body. This is surely the ultimate sanction – controlling what we do with our bodies, including sex, in order to 'glorify God in our bodies'.

Is this how it is with you? Or is your body no more than a workshop, a clothes-hanger, a mobile loudspeaker, a machine, a misshapen absorber of edibles? As in pagan

Corinth, the view in Western culture may veer between the glorification of the perfect body – promoted in fashion magazines and media advertising – and dissatisfaction that our bodies fail to live up to this impossible ideal. The result, as touched on earlier, is that disorders like anorexia and bulimia nervosa are becoming increasingly widespread, and we spend a lot of money on cosmetics and on long sessions in the gym.

Paul gives the argument a further twist. We are inclined to blame the body and its passions for leading us into trouble and for the sins we so easily succumb to. But Paul sees the body as subject to the demands we make on *it* (6:18b). The impulse to sin comes from within us, from the 'heart' (Matt 15:19): the body is governed by the response we make to that impulse. 'Therefore honour God with your body'.

For reflection

- Paul tackles the difficult question of how the community of believers should deal with individuals inside and outside the church who do not share their strict moral standards (1 Cor 5:9–11). He defines the boundaries they should observe. Can you re-state them in your own words and in a form that would make sense to the culture in which you live?

- 'The very fact that you have lawsuits among you means you have been completely defeated already. Why not rather be wronged? Why not rather be cheated?' (1 Cor 6:7). But should we *always* refuse to take counter-action when we are wronged?

- 'You are not your own; you were bought at a price. Therefore honour God with your body' (1 Cor 6:20). Think about your own lifestyle. What are the practical implications of this statement for you?

MARRIAGE, DIVORCE AND CHRISTIAN PRIORITIES

1 Corinthians 7

Paul now begins to address specific issues mentioned by the church in their letter to him (1 Cor 7:1). His teaching on marriage and divorce reveals the danger of adopting simplistic attitudes and dealing with complex issues like sexuality as if they were 'black-and-white'. 'God has called us to live in peace' (v 15b) – this maxim should override oppressively legalistic interpretations of the law (eg Matt 12:1–8). While we may want to give a clear message about the importance of abiding by moral boundaries, human relationships are always complex. Defining a balanced position is particularly difficult in matters of sexuality where powerful unconscious influences are at work. Mercy, understanding and grace are vital ingredients in the work of bringing human sexuality under God's influence.

To understand this section we should keep in mind as we read what Paul has already said about the body being God's temple and the need to honour him in the way we use our bodies (1 Cor 6:19–20). Much of his teaching was made with the view that he was giving advice for a purely temporary situation (7:26, 31). He frequently says that he is not giving 'commands from God' but rather his considered opinion as God's apostle (7:6, 12, 25, 35, 40) out of his concern to help those for whom he was responsible, fulfilling his role as their pastor and 'father in the gospel'.

Some reading this chapter may see it as a totally negative, legalistic list of rules and regulations on the subject of sexuality. But Paul is addressing tensions that were being felt by people living in a particularly immoral kind of culture. (It was while he was in Corinth that he wrote his searing indictment of moral standards in the pagan world, Rom 1:28–32 – a reaction perhaps to the immoral life in the city.) He is well aware of the pressures that emanated from the culture in which the Corinthians lived. 'So much immorality' (1 Cor 7:2, NIV) is actually spelt out much more precisely in the Greek as 'so many fornications' (plural). In Corinth, sexual promiscuity was the order of the day. Although the Corinthians did not have a tabloid press to draw attention to this kind of behaviour, they had the temple of Aphrodite where ritual prostitution gave religious sanction to such indulgence. In this kind of environment Paul's rather blunt advice to the church that unless they had the gift of celibacy 'each man should have his own wife, and each woman her own husband' makes very good sense.

Marriage: the norm for Christians

A very confusing situation seems to have arisen. There were groups in the church whose hedonistic attitude to life is summed up in the phrase 'Everything is permissible to me' (6:12): but now Paul seems to be addressing those who have gone to the other extreme and are emphasising the need to *deny* the passions of the flesh altogether and to abstain from what they see as carnal self-indulgence. The sentence 'It is good for a man not to marry' (7:1) may well be a direct quotation from the leaders' original letter to the apostle.

Paul sees marriage as the norm for God's people, and this should include regular love-making (v 3). His view of the marital relationship is in some ways ahead of his time: husband and wife have equal responsibility in ensuring that the other is happy and satisfied within the relationship (vs 4–5). In Corinthian society outside the church the husband had complete rights over his wife's body, she having very little say in the matter. But in a Christian marriage, sexual intercourse is a mutual act, a sacrament of

mutuality in fact – and there is no suggestion of one partner enforcing his or her rights over the other, whether it be
the right to sexual intercourse or the right to abstinence.

Paul is a realist and sensitive to the human condition.
Though he himself prefers celibacy, he recognises that
celibacy is a gift and places it among the other gifts from
God, using the same word to describe it ('charismata',
v 7). He realises that the majority of human beings will
find greater completeness in marriage (11:11), even those
in similar circumstances to himself (9:5). He does not
command a celibate life for those who cannot sustain it,
nor does he say that being celibate is superior to being
married. As with the other gifts, celibacy is entirely at
God's disposal. So it is not enough to feel that we have a
'vocation' to celibacy. If we are wrong we may well find
ourselves in trouble.

The fact is that in our culture, as in the Corinthian one,
sex is virtually worshipped. To be in a sexual relationship
– casual or committed, inside or outside marriage – is
taken for granted as normal, and to be celibate is to be
unusual or even 'weird'. There is pressure on people to
have a number of sexual partners rather than to stick to
one. We get advice on how to have good, safe sex rather
than how to make good, strong relationships. Indeed,
sometimes in the loneliness of modern life it seems that the
only way an individual can find intimacy is to be involved
with another person sexually. Those not in relationships
may feel isolated and devalued by the society around them
which seems to operate on the assumption that every individual is half of a couple. But whether we have never been
married, whether we have been widowed or divorced, we
are still whole people. This may be of some comfort to the
many unmarried Christians today who do not feel they
have the gift of celibacy, but are 'stuck' in a particular situation: their faith prevents them from attaching
themselves to someone who is not a Christian; yet they
have not found an appropriate marriage partner within
the church. The longing for community is part of the

reflection of God's image in us; it does not arise because we are all one half of a whole looking for the other half.

Paul appears to make little room for divorce (7:10–11) which, he says (and this from the Lord), has no place in God's original scheme (Mark 10:9; Luke 16:18). But this does not make divorce an unforgivable sin any more than adultery or oath-taking which, like Paul, Jesus also prohibited (Matt 5:27–37).

One widely accepted Christian teaching is that marriage is a 'creation ordinance' (Gen 2:24): therefore *all* marriages are equally binding in the sight of God, whether or not the partners acknowledge him. There is of course an element of truth in this. However, Paul is taking into account God's grace and human failure. He assumes his role as a pastor (1 Cor 7:12a) and now goes on to set out a more compassionate view (vs 12b–16) than he at first adopted in verses 10 and 11. If the partner in the marriage who is not a Christian wishes to abandon it when their spouse is converted, they can do so (vs 15). This 'let out' went some way towards alleviating the situation of a Christian wife whose pagan husband was actively ill-treating her because of her new-found faith. But if the two are willing to stay together, then this is the best possible outcome.

And those of us married to someone who does not share our faith can be encouraged – Paul backs up his view with the rather beautiful thought that the believing partner may well be a source of sanctification and salvation for the unbelieving spouse (vs 14, 16). This effect even extends to any children the couple may have. So often we view this the other way around and worry about the negative effect unbelievers may be having on Christians.

'Remain in your situation'

In verses 17–24 the discussion broadens away from marriage to take in an individual's general circumstances. The verses seem to imply that Paul is discouraging something which we might consider to be perfectly reasonable – the desire to alter one's condition in life.

Whether or not a new male convert to Christianity followed the Jewish custom and was circumcised had been a cause for hot debate among the early Christians. The division between converts from Judaism and converts from among the Gentiles was one of the big social divisions in the church. Paul, who saw himself as the apostle to the Gentiles, came down clearly on the side of the view that it was not an option (vs 18–19; see Acts 15:1–29; Gal 5:2 *ff*). For him obedience to God was more important than fulfilling cultural and religious observances. With the fundamental break between the old covenant and the new one inaugurated by Jesus, the mark of circumcision became unnecessary. In general, it is probably sensible that those newly come to faith do not plunge into a wholesale series of life changes while they are adjusting to life as a believer (except, of course, in matters involving moral right and wrong). New Christians need time to assimilate their new-found faith and establish a steady pattern of committed discipleship before making other big decisions.

However, as with divorce, Paul allows an exception to his general argument and, again, it is a case of seeking to alleviate the circumstances of someone who was socially powerless. If a slave could buy his freedom, he should do so (1 Cor 7:21). Slavery formed the other big social division within the church. A slave's life depended very much on how he was treated by his master. If someone found himself trapped in an intolerable situation, it would have been unreasonable not to allow him to obtain his freedom if he could. Nevertheless, in Paul's view once a slave became a Christian, he became free: and the man who had been free became Christ's slave. In effect they were both free of men and slaves of Christ, because Christ had redeemed (ie 'bought') them from slavery to sin (v 23). In God's eyes, the act of conversion broke down the distinction between them. This knowledge, of course, should affect the way Christian slave-owners treated the slaves in their care (Eph 6:9; Philemon 15–16).

Slavery is rare today (though it still exists in some parts of the world), and we may not view Paul's advice as something that can readily apply to us. However, relationships between ourselves and those in authority over us are an important part of our lives, particularly in the workplace. Whatever our circumstances, we can take on board Paul's general principle that we should not give in to the desire to scramble up the ladder of success, stepping on others on the way, or take advantage of our powerful position to exploit others (such as in doctor-patient, lawyer-client or teacher-pupil relationships). Nor should we be envious of, or disgruntled with, those in authority over us. Our behaviour towards each other should be governed by the knowledge that we 'were bought at a price; [so] do not become slaves of men'. Our social standing, the kind of jobs we do, whether we are at the top or bottom of the heap, married or unmarried – does not, finally, matter. What does matter is *how* we live and whether or not we allow God's authority over us to affect how we treat other people.

So Paul is not closing the door on altering our circumstances or developing our skills and abilities, so long as this is part of gaining maturity in our faith and growing in God's service. If our personal situation *is* hindering our relationship with God, then it is worth considering if and how we could change it for the better. But, on the whole, we should try not to worry about our personal circumstances and entrust them to God. This, of course, is easier said than done in a competitive world where to opt out of the race may be costly in terms of wealth, job prospects and the opportunities open to us. However, we should not be embarrassed to be distinctive as God's people, and our witness is authenticated if we are seen to be living by what we believe. There are probably many people outside the church who would welcome a stand against the materialism and the preoccupation with status that exists in our world. These people may be drawn to Christ by authentic Christian lifestyles.

Apostolic authority and eternal values

At verse 25 we enter into a particularly difficult passage, about which there is a good deal of controversy. In his Tyndale Commentary, Leon Morris takes eight pages of closely reasoned discussion and argument to suggest how many variations of viewpoint there are. For example, the word Paul uses for 'marry' (v 38, Greek *gamizo*) is an unusual one and it is hard to determine its precise meaning. According to Leon Morris this raises several questions, all of which remain unanswered! Verses 32–36 appear to contradict general Christian teaching that marriage is a sacrament instituted by God, and is at odds with Paul's teaching elsewhere that the marital relationship is a reflection of that between Christ and his church (Eph 5:22–26).

Paul is responding to particular issues arising from the problems in the church (1 Cor 7:25, 36–40), and we do not know enough about local customs and practices of the time to form any clear picture of what he means by 'virgins' (vs 25, 28, 34, 37–38). Nor do we have a full account of the questions that were raised on the subject by the ascetic party at Corinth. One suggestion put forward to explain the references to 'virgins' is that some of the Corinthian believers, unhappy with the idea of full marital relationships, were attempting to practise a kind of 'marriage-without-sex' where women lived with their husbands as 'spiritual sisters' – a way of life that was later advocated by a well-known third-century Christian leader, Tertullian. However, bearing in mind Paul's earlier comment about celibacy being a gift and the realities of human nature, it was probably unlikely that these couples were handling these platonic relationships very well! Whatever the case, Paul is looking at the matter from a much wider perspective than whether or not sexual relations are appropriate within marriage.

Though he claims to be speaking with a distinctive form of authority, in this instance Paul admits that he has no direct teaching from the Lord (v 25, although on other occasions he did – eg v 10; Gal 1:12*ff*). This admission allows us to be cautious in our understanding of what he is saying. The phrase – 'the time is short' (1 Cor 7:29) – has been explained in a variety of ways: some commentators think that Paul is referring to the Second Coming; Calvin saw in it a reference to the brevity of life; others relate it to the 'distress' resulting from the 'present crisis' (v 26), possibly a famine or Roman persecution. Paul was writing to a church in a city under Roman authority and the persecution of Christians was already beginning. Life in Corinth was undoubtedly volatile, and the apostle wanted to give practical, appropriate counsel to those who were living in the midst of it all.

In verses 26–31 he continues to push home his point that Christians should be content to remain as they are, especially in the light of their eternal future. Paul always had one eye on eternity (see also 2 Cor 5:16–18) and was always ready for the world as he knew it to come to an end; he tended to view life in the light of this expectation. So we sense that he is not setting down hard and fast rules, even though he has firm convictions of his own as to what is desirable. All Christian decision-making should be controlled by the over-ruling principle that 'our citizenship is in heaven' (Phil 3:20). We are destined for eternity and this not only helps us to endure hardship (2 Cor 4:16–17) but also to 'sit loose' to the pains and the pleasures of this passing world. While marriage is a glorious expression of the spiritual union of Christ with his people, with the potential to be one of the deepest of human relationships, it is not the be-all and end-all of life; it is desirable but not mandatory. Marriage won't exist in heaven (Mark 12:25), but will instead be replaced by other relationships in which we will find all the intimacy and fulfilment that we could desire – something we can all look forward to with joyful anticipation, whether we are married or single.

But now, observe, everlasting considerations are to come in, not to sadden joy but to calm it ... we are to be calm, cheerful, self-possessed; to sit loose to all these sources of enjoyment, masters of ourselves.

(F W Robertson)

For reflection

- If you are married to someone who is not a Christian, reflect on your relationship with your spouse in the light of the following verses.

    'Do you not know that your body is a temple of the Holy Spirit, who is in you, whom you have received from God?' (1 Cor 6:19).

    'The wife's body does not belong to her alone but also to her husband. In the same way, the husband's body does not belong to him alone but also to his wife' (1 Cor 7:4).

    'For the unbelieving husband has been sanctified through his wife, and the unbelieving wife has been sanctified through her believing husband' (1 Cor 7:14).

- How do you think it is possible for someone who is unmarried to know that they have the gift of celibacy? How does our faith help us cope if we are 'unhappily unmarried'?

- 'Each man should remain in the situation which he was in when God called him' (1 Cor 7:20). What might this verse mean for Christians in terms of seeking promotion or to improve themselves?

    Is there something in your own situation you would like to change? Work out how you might do this in the light of Paul's teaching.

RESOLVING A TRICKY PROBLEM –
AT THE CROSS

1 Corinthians 8

Coming from a world where materialism and scientific rationalism are the dominant forces shaping our attitudes (though this is changing), we are apt to regard the pagan idolatry that characterised the environment of the early church as remote from our own situation. None of us are in danger, we feel, of worshipping a carved wooden object. But in saying this, we may well have missed the point. Behind the facade of rationalism in our world, paganism is alive and well, and does not depend on the presence or absence of visible idols. The following could be a fair description of the beliefs that lie behind the Gaia theory, New Age beliefs, astrology, even creation theology:

> To the pagan mind, nature was alive with divine presences, linked to them in rhythms that were cosmic and spiritual...they viewed dreams as a special means of access to this reality...intuition and imagination, not to mention dreams, were considered far more potent as vehicles of knowledge than reason...
> (*No Place for Truth*, David Wells, p 265.)

Superstition is alive and well in many parts of the world today, including the sophisticated, cosmopolitan West! The world of the enlightenment, with its emphasis on reason, is giving way to a surge of beliefs in the supernatural and in the presence of the divine in nature. Paganism, which never really disappeared in many places, is gaining ground again in Britain. There are those who still worship objects – natural or man-made – in which they perceive divine influences.

And people are adopting a less mechanistic, more holistic view of how the world and its ecosystems operate in intricate, organic harmony. Much of this has arisen out of concern for the environment and greater understanding of the web of delicate balances in nature that are so easily upset by unthinking human activity. Many view with horror the way human greed, ignorance and even desperation caused by poverty have led to the destruction of our beautiful planet. Christians are becoming increasingly unhappy about the way scripture has been used in the past to justify the appalling exploitation of the world's resources.

This move away from the rational has encouraged a more creative attitude to science. The relationship between matter and anti-matter, the alleged discovery of primitive life forms on Mars and the prospect of life elsewhere in the universe, the mapping out of our genetic code, how everything began in the first place – all this has opened up seemingly limitless possibilities for human endeavour in which both reason and the imagination have a place. The church can learn from these new ways of thinking, in particular the concern for the environment, and allowing the imagination as much space as reason in the way we approach scripture and worship. However, when these ideas dominate all other considerations, when they override our responsibility to other people, when they take the place of God in our lives, they become idolatry.

Perhaps we should pause to consider what the term 'idolatry' actually means. Idolatry can be defined as the excessive adulation of any person or object, so that we allow that person or object to gain total ascendancy over our lives. Everything we do, think and say is done, thought or said in the light of that person or object. Excessive adulation can be extended beyond concrete images to take in abstract ideas and ideologies which we make into idols and try to appease in the same way that primitive societies once tried to appease the gods of nature.

Idols – nonentities to be taken seriously

Many idols were on show around the streets of Corinth, and their predominance in the city's culture and commerce made it impossible for the Christian believer to avoid all contact. For the poor, especially in times of famine, the temple feasts were an important source of food, particularly the sacrificial meat which provided rare but necessary protein. Much of the meat from sacrifices was in any case later sold in the market, and it was difficult to avoid buying it. A tradesman in Corinth would have to belong to the appropriate trade guild, and these guilds would hold meetings and celebrations in the temples, possibly incorporating elements of idol-worship. And in a Roman colony the cult of emperor worship was particularly strongly enforced.

The Jewish community had been forced to come to terms with idolatry and had faced the same dilemma that the Corinthian church faced now. In the view of the rabbis, statues of gods and goddesses were to be regarded as ornaments, not gods. There is an account that once, when some Jews were seen pouring water over themselves in the bath of Aphrodite and were challenged by a rabbi, another rabbi replied that the waters were public property and could not be forbidden by virtue of their being a pagan sanctum. A Jewish workman was permitted to make an idol for a customer provided he did not bow down to it himself.

Before he gets down to the nitty-gritty of how to deal with this problem, Paul establishes an important principle (1 Cor 8:1–2). Whenever we approach a potential source of trouble, we should have the view that no matter how much we know (or think we know) the truth, or how much we feel that we are in the right, our response should be founded on love. When we think like this, we are closest to God's heart, and God is in us (v 3; John 15:9–12; 17:26). There is, in fact, something more important going on than a correct understanding of doctrine. Anticipating what he will say later on in his letter (1 Cor 13:2) Paul insists that *love,* not knowledge, is the key both to knowing God and to being known by him.

Paul contrasts the worship of idols with the Christian faith in the one true God who is *both* Father and Son (8:4–6); for him there is no question of there being separate divine entities living side by side with each other. Therefore, an idol has no personal reality and no power. For some in the church this was not a problem: an idol was a 'nothing' – they knew and worshipped the one true and living God. Meat from the temples was no different from meat from any other source (v 8); and if they were invited to join in a feast at the temple, they were happy to do so provided they did nothing that might be interpreted as worshipping the idol itself.

But for others in the church it was not so simple. Having once worshipped idols, they were aware of the powerful hold they exerted and could not dismiss them so readily (v 7). Indeed this 'power' was one to be reckoned with. In addition to phenomena like 'speaking in tongues' and 'prophesying', which were regularly experienced in the pagan temples, there were more impressive happenings. One Jewish writer of the period, advising Jewish believers on this problem, commented, 'Nevertheless, we see men enter the shrine crippled and come out cured,' referring to the healing that occurred in the temples of Aesculapius and Serapis. Similar phenomena take place in spiritualist and New Age circles in our own day, and pose similar questions. It seems that there is a power in the world that can ape the activities of the Spirit, and discernment is needed to see what is truly from God and what isn't (1 John 4:1–6).

There is no doubt about Paul's personal convictions in the matter. At the doctrinal and intellectual level his sympathies are with the 'an idol is nothing' group. But he is sensitive to the scruples of those who cannot adopt such a clear-cut, intellectual stance and whose consciences are genuinely troubled. The conflict here is not between the 'weak' and the 'strong', but between those who 'know' – who are intellectually aware and can see that an idol is nothing – and those who feel that there is something intrinsically wrong with *any* link with idolatry. His pastoral heart enables him to see why some believers have scruples. In his own words, 'the love of Christ constrained' him (2 Cor 5:14). He will not insist on 'doing right' if this means upsetting the faith of another believer.

Following the law of love

The potential for trouble can be great. For example, some Christians think listening to rock music is fine, it's just another form of cultural expression; others will have scruples about the lyrics. Some will see no harm in going to rave parties or clubs – after all, they are opportunities for meeting non-Christians on neutral ground; others will worry about what this has to say about the distinctiveness of Christianity. Some will think smoking is just another social habit, OK in moderation; others will regard it as abusing God's temple (1 Cor 6:19). Where can the boundaries be established?

If the life of a Christian fellowship is controlled by the priority of love, there will be little scope for the devil (who relishes intellectual argument) to intrude into its affairs. However, there is a snag. Following the 'law of love' involves the risk that the 'weaker' brother or sister will exact a kind of emotional blackmail to get their own way. Following the way of love makes very great demands on us, and calls for exceptional maturity if it is not to lead to people being abused or exploited.

Following the way of love may upset a credo that lies very close to our hearts – the business of establishing and claiming our 'rights'. In terms of 'rights' the 'weaker' brother' (8:11) had no case; the believer with 'knowledge' was correct to assert that an idol was 'nothing' and he had every right to go to the guild-festival in the temple and share in the feasting. But, as we see later in chapter 9, Paul will not even insist on his own rights as an apostle, and he urges the believers at Corinth to follow his example (4:16). The Christian church is a community in which the popular assumptions about the matter of 'rights' have no control over our behaviour. The cry 'You have a right to do this or have that' cannot dominate our thinking; instead we should exercise judgement and base our decisions on the effects they will have on others. This will, of course, mean a lot of pain. It is hard to forego what we know to be right, and even harder to give way to the objections and, as they seem to us, prejudices of other people. This is another example of 'dying to self' and trusting God that he will work in the hearts of 'weaker' Christians – or indeed in our own!

Once again, as so often in this letter, Paul takes his readers to the place where all such matters are to be resolved – the cross. That 'weaker' Christian, whose objections were to be over-ridden, was not simply an immature, ill-taught, awkward believer: he was a 'brother for whom Christ died' (8:11). If Christ thought he was worth dying for, then a fellow-believer could certainly go without a favourite cut of meat for his sake. All our relationships within the church are subject to the same constraint. We are dealing with people for whom Christ died. And if that is not enough, we remember Jesus' teaching (Matt 25:40, 45) that what we do to others we actually do to him. In short, Christians do not operate only in a credal framework – concerned for truth, as Bruce Winter puts it – but in a relational one: we should be concerned for one another. And if we have to grade these in order of importance, it is the relational and not the credal which comes first – 'the greatest of these is love' (1 Cor 13:13).

For reflection

- 'Knowledge puffs up, but love builds up' (1 Cor 8:1). Is there anything that you consider permissible but which you know could offend or upset other

Christians in your fellowship? Reflect on how you are managing the difficult balance between 'knowledge' and 'love'.

- 'Be careful, however, that the exercise of your freedom does not become a stumbling-block to the weak' (1 Cor 8:9).

  Are there any limits to the principle laid down in this verse? Don't the 'weak' have a responsibility to acknowledge the truth behind the actions of the 'strong', and bring their consciences into line? Or does the consideration that they are people 'for whom Christ died' overrule every other consideration?

APOSTOLIC LIVING AND
APOSTOLIC MOTIVATION

1 Corinthians 9

Paul continues his argument that rights should not be asserted to the detriment of others. Previously he had made the point that Christians should not always insist on their 'rights' (1 Cor 8:12–13): there is something more important at stake – the gospel. Now he supports his case by pointing out that he himself has not always insisted on his own rights as an apostle (9:12, 15).

The explosion of rhetorical questions (vs 1–8) shows how strongly Paul felt about his apostolic status and the rights that went with it. He gives the Corinthians a list of rights he has deliberately not insisted on so as not to hinder the progress of the gospel (vs 4–6). He was so strongly determined not to damage his witness to Jesus Christ (v 12), he made tents (Acts 18:3) when he might have been demanding – as the Jewish rabbis and priests, and the other apostles did – that his converts supported him (1 Cor 9:9–11).

Some might have accused him of seeking personal gain if he took the Corinthians' money; others might have said that he was spurning their offers of help. Some of the church factions may also have been saying that his willingness to give up his right to their support meant that his ministry was inferior. Members of the 'Peter party' may even have been disputing his right to be an apostle at all, because he had not been one of the Twelve who accompanied Jesus during his ministry and witnessed the resurrection. If their aim was to impose Jewish-style legalism on the young church, they would regard this as a powerful argument. Missionaries and Christian leaders often find themselves in 'no-win' situations like this, where the only thing that sustains them in the end is their own inner integrity before God.

But Paul insists that he is doubly qualified. He *had* 'met the Lord', which was the formal test (Acts 1:21–2; 9:1a, 5). But even more to the point, he had shown that he was an apostle at Corinth by founding the church there (1 Cor 9:1b; see also Rom 15:15–21).

Paul uses his Bible

Paul defends his right to support from the church in two ways: first, by analogy with accepted human experience – the soldier, the vine-grower and the herdsman who all live by their labours (1 Cor 9:7); second, by referring to scripture. It is significant that he does it this way: we might have expected him to go to scripture first to find support for his authority. But sound reasoning is a gift of God and should carry due weight in Christian discussion.

We may also wonder about the scriptures he chooses to support his case (v 9; see Deut 25:4; 1 Tim 5:18) – they don't seem to have any direct bearing on the issue. However, they illustrate his principle and this is what matters. Scripture may be usefully interpreted when we cannot find any direct guidance on a situation. We can draw principles from biblical references which will give us sufficient guidance if we seek it wisely. The command referred to in verse 14 is generally taken to refer to Jesus' direction to the disciples when he sent them out ahead of him to minister in the towns and villages of Galilee (Luke 10:7): 'Stay in that house, eating and drinking whatever they give you, for the worker deserves his wages'.

Verses 15–19 call to mind Martin Luther's dictum: 'A Christian man is the most free lord of all, subject to none. A Christian man is the most dutiful servant of all, subject to all' (*Liberty of a Christian Man*). All true disciples have to live with this apparent paradox, and we are bound to have problems as we try to reconcile the two halves of this statement. It is a development of Paul's earlier argument that 'he who was a slave when he was called by the Lord is the Lord's freedman; similarly, he who was a free man when he was called is Christ's slave' (1 Cor 7:22): yet we must 'be careful, however, that the exercise of [our] freedom does not become a stumbling block to the weak' (8:9). So we have the paradox of our freedom in Christ; and yet, as his slaves, we must obey his command to 'Love one another' which means that we also serve (John 13:12–17).

Paul is free to choose not to take money from the Corinthians and to work for his living instead. For him, this was something to 'boast' about (1 Cor 9:15). But when it comes to preaching the gospel, he has no freedom of choice whatsoever (v 16). He *has* to preach – it is a trust committed to him by his Lord. This is reminiscent of Jeremiah's complaint: '...if I say, "I will not mention him or speak any more in his name," his word is in my heart like a fire, a fire shut up in my bones. I am weary of holding it in; indeed, I cannot' (Jer 20:9).

Living under the law of Christ

While some in the Corinthian church criticised Paul for not being Jewish enough and for living like a Gentile (1 Cor 9:21), others may have criticised him for giving in to Jewish scruples (v 20), even to the point of taking a Nazirite vow (Acts 21:23*ff*). The clause in brackets – 'though I am not free from God's law but am under Christ's law' – shows him taking special care not to be misunderstood by those who seemed to be taking their 'freedom' to mean 'freedom from any restraint whatsoever'.

In recent years, when there has been a strong reaction against 'legalism', this distinction has not always been made clear, and the result has been confusion and controversy. For the Christian believer the Jewish code with its 613 written rules is not compulsory. The law came into being because of sin, but through it also came God's judgement (Gal 3:10, 19). While rules and regulations have the power to control human wickedness and make us aware of boundaries we should not cross (Rom 3:20), they cannot prevent us from sinning nor can they cleanse sin from the human heart (Rom 7:14–24; Gal 3:21). Only Christ can do this (1 John 1:7–9) and we are free from the law's judgement only by faith in him, and not by the way we observe the law (Gal 5:2–6). Christ, therefore, fulfils the law for those who call on his name' (Matt 5:17; Luke 24:44) and to them he becomes the law.

We need to be clear what being under 'Christ's law' really means. Christ summarises the law thus: ' "Love the Lord your God with all your heart and with all your soul and with all your mind ... Love your neighbour as yourself." All the Law and the Prophets hand on these two commandments' (Matt 22:40). This concept of 'love' can easily degenerate merely into being 'a nice person', an assumption commonly made about the way Christians behave. However, Christ did not come to found a code of ethics or rules for life, but to establish a relationship – with himself, under the guidance of the Holy Spirit. The Gospels provide us with specific commands from Christ for those who want to follow him, and over and above them is set his own example. Paul himself shows us how we can put Christ's summary of the law into practice (Rom 13:8–10; Gal 6:2).

The phrase 'the law of Christ' raises very important questions. Some would say that it is a contradiction. Didn't Christ came to deliver us from 'the terrors of the Law', whereas Moses set down a set of rules that were all negative in intention? Didn't Jesus come to open up a 'way' characterised by love? Haven't the tablets of stone from Sinai been replaced by the truths set out in the Sermon on the Mount which are largely relational in intent, and focused on the command to love God, one's neighbour and even one's enemies (Matt 5:17–20)? However, as Jesus explained, he was not so much replacing the law as bringing out its true meaning by fulfilling its demands through his death. The law of Moses was written on stone: but the law of Christ is written in our hearts, and thus has the power to affect our wills and intentions.

There is a further dimension:

> And so he condemned sin in sinful man, in order that the righteous requirements of the law might be fully met in us, who do not live according to the sinful nature but according to the Spirit.
>
> Those who live according to the sinful nature have their minds set on what that nature desires; but those who live in accordance with the Spirit have their minds set on what the Spirit desires. The mind of sinful man is death, but the mind controlled by the Spirit is life and peace; the sinful mind is hostile to God. It does not submit to God's law, nor can it do so. Those controlled by the sinful nature cannot please God.
>
> You, however, are controlled not by the sinful nature but by the Spirit, if the Spirit of God lives in you.
>
> (Romans 8:4–9)

Paul takes us deep into the heart of true religion, which is not so much about what we do but *how* we do it. The Holy Spirit in the heart provides the power to know how we should act as well as helping us to see how Christ's law can operate in us. In doing so the Spirit makes Christ real to us:

> The man without the Spirit does not accept the things that come from the Spirit of God, for they are foolishness to him, and he cannot understand them, because they are spiritually discerned. The spiritual man makes judgments about all things, but he himself is not subject to an man's judgment.
>
> 'For who has known the mind of the Lord that he may instruct him?'
>
> But we have the mind of Christ.
>
> (1 Corinthians 2:14–16)

The formula, 'all things to all men' (1 Cor 9:22–23) could be regarded as a formula for trouble. Certainly it fitted in with Paul's aim – 'by all possible means[to] save some'; but equally it could be said to guarantee that by those same means he would offend others. How would he know where to draw the line? It called for very clear vision on his part of what he was aiming to do, a total absence of personal ambition and deep integrity in his walk with God.

Christ also offended many when he mixed with those they regarded as prostitutes and sinners. Christians may face the same difficulty when they try to seek those whom others in the church may regard as 'not respectable'. But it is here that Christ's love is truly demonstrated. Tony Campolo tells of how circumstances led him on one occasion to join with the regulars at an American bar in arranging a birthday surprise for a depressed and lonely prostitute: he was rightly working to the same principle of love. There will always be differences of opinion about how far a Christian should go.

Following Christ's law is bound to put us in difficult situations, if only because that law cannot be written down in absolute terms and is more concerned with what 'thou shalt' do rather than with what 'thou shalt not'! A fully defined code like the Jewish law, with its precise rulings and prohibitions, has its problems, but in fact is easier to live with. Many prefer to follow rules than form relationships which have the potential to be difficult, with people they wouldn't normally connect with. Whether we assert our rights and privileges, whether we have 'knowledge' and are clear on doctrine, whether we follow the law or exercise freedom in Christ, all these are of no value if they don't lead to loving fruitful relationships with people inside and outside the church.

Obeying 'the law of Christ' calls for spiritual maturity and personal discipline of a high order, which is why Paul continues this chapter as he does, by talking about self-control.

Vandalising the temple

Verses 24–27 call for stern and costly self-discipline, particularly in relation to the temptations of the flesh – and they are by no means all to do with sex. The widespread manifestations of eating disorders, problems with drink and drugs, our violent and selfish treatment of each other, are all symptomatic of our inability to exercise self-control.

The Isthmian Games were held near Corinth, and Paul's chosen analogy between Christian self-discipline and the strict training and competitive spirit of the athlete would have made a direct appeal to those he was writing to. The ideal body and its beauty were revered in Greek culture. Athleticism was especially highly regarded, and athletes were willing to train hard and to go through strenuous self-denial and strict training to fulfil their desire to win. According to Paul, this kind of dedication for so fleeting a prize (v 25) should put the Corinthians to shame. The Christian's prize 'will last for ever' and is of infinite value. Surely working at their faith is more than worthy of their time and effort.

Self-control is the forgotten dimension of what used to be called 'sanctification' or holy living. In traditional evangelical teaching, the emphasis was put on the need for the Holy Spirit to work in us to make us holy and Christlike – 'refining fire, go through my heart, and sanctify the whole' as Wesley put it. 'Convention teaching' seemed to imply that any effort we made towards our own spiritual development – from hair shirts to track suits, so to speak! – was a hindrance to the power of the Holy Spirit. So we find ourselves going down the same track as those Greek philosophers, sinking into a kind of spiritual quietism. In a classic 'Convention' hymn, the writer puts it thus:

> The self I cannot conquer, the will that still is mine,
> Oh, take them both, Lord Jesus, and make them one
>   with Thine

> Take them! I cannot yield them – I am not what I
>   seemed,
> I have no power, Lord Jesus, to do what once I dreamed
> The yearning of the earth-life is stronger than my
>   strength,
> When may the spell be broken, and freedom come at
>   length!

Paul insists otherwise. There is much we can and should do, which will demand plenty of will power and 'won't' power. While the Holy Spirit does have overall control of our spiritual development, we have no right just to sit back and expect him to do it all. The words Paul uses are very forceful – 'beat' (v 27) translates a verb that comes from the boxing ring, meaning 'give a black eye to' – and he makes his body a 'slave'. He is not afraid that he will lose his salvation (3:15), but he is afraid of being 'disqualified for the prize', the 'crown' (1 Pet 5:4; Rev 2:10b). Taking control of the outworking of his faith is part and parcel of his calling as an evangelist.

Exercising self-control, both spiritually and physically, is part of the process of demonstrating love for others. It is self-control which enables us to be willing to forego rights and privileges for the sake of others, and to persevere when times are rough. The challenge is to resist any indulgence of fleshly appetites and the belief that to be a Christian does not require hard work in prayer, service and striving for godly attitudes. This way of thinking makes for 'flabby Christians', useless in the great struggle 'by all possible means [to] save some'. Self-control is also good for us in terms of health and fitness, and there is nothing wrong in having space in our lives for exercise and taking care of our bodies: God made them and he wants us to take reasonable care of them. We have already noted that in these days of holistic medicine, body and spirit are seen as an integrated whole, and it is recognised that the health of the one affects the health of the other. So the target for self-control is the body, not because it is inherently evil but because through it bodily appetites can corrupt spirituality. When we remember that the body is the temple of the Holy Spirit (6:19) we should recognise that to neglect, abuse or pamper it is vandalism – like going round Westminster Abbey with a spray paint can and writing graffiti over the monuments.

In the relative luxury of the West, it is very easy to overindulge. But self-indulgence of any kind – whether it be overeating, drinking too much or being lazy about our prayer-life – must be brought 'captive' to Christ (2 Cor 10:5) if we are to be effective in our Christian calling. If we don't take the gospel seriously enough to control our appetites, we are not likely to take it seriously enough to want to persuade others to believe.

For reflection

• 'On the contrary, we put up with anything...' (1 Cor 9:12).

   Absolutely anything? Are there no limits to what God's servants should endure at the hands of others? If there is a limit, how can we know when it has been reached?

• 'Everyone who competes in the games goes into strict training...' (1 Cor 9:25). What does this really mean for the committed believer? What does it mean for you? Spell out your answer in practical terms.

THE TIMELESS WORD

1 Corinthians 10:1–13

Paul does not suddenly switch over to a new subject. The first word 'For' (1 Cor 10:1) is a connecting word, so what follows is a logical next step in his theme of taking the Christian life seriously so as not to drift in our faith and thus find ourselves disqualified from the prize that God holds in keeping for us (9:27). To reinforce this point, Paul turns to incidents in the history of God's people Israel when they were on their journey to the promised land. The shock is that the majority of them behaved so disobediently they never arrived.

What is particularly interesting is the way Paul identifies Christians so directly with the Old Testament people of God. 'Our forefathers,' he says – addressing a Gentile audience no differently from a purely Jewish one. This is in line with his teaching in Romans 11:17–21, where he talks of Gentile believers being 'grafted in' to the Jewish 'tree' and warns the Christians not to forget that God had come to them through Israel. This does not mean that we need accept Judaism as a 'sister faith'. Nevertheless, we should honour the Jews for what God has done through them for us, and we have a debt to them (Rom 10:1, 14–15).

It may help us get the thrust of Paul's teaching if we put single quotation marks round the words 'baptised', 'food', 'drink' and 'rock' (1 Cor 10:2–4). The experiences of Old Testament Israel prefigured the experiences of Christians. Passing through the Red Sea prefigured baptism; eating the manna and drinking the water prefigured Holy Communion (according to Calvin and others, though not all are agreed on this). The most striking analogy is in the word 'rock'. Twice in their wilderness journey – early on (Exod 17) and towards the end (Num 20) – the Lord refreshed his people with 'water from the rock'. This gave rise to a Jewish legend that a literal rock had travelled with them all through the desert to provide water. Paul improves on this story by using the rock to prefigure Christ, the one who gives the 'living water' of his Spirit (John 4:13) to his people all through their earthly pilgrimage. But, as he says, sharing in these outward and visible experiences did not guarantee Israel's spiritual well-being (1 Cor 10:5) or protect them from the consequences of their misdeeds. In the same way, taking part in the Christian sacraments and rites of passage will not protect Christians from the consequences of their sins or guarantee them entry into that final bliss.

Follies not to be repeated

The experiences of Israel hold lessons for us (v 6). They are a warning against being so confident in our position as Christians that we put ourselves deliberately in the way of temptation. Note that the illustrations Paul uses are all the follies and sins of Old Testament times. Idolatry and self-indulgence (v 7; Exod 32:6), immorality (v 8; Num 25:1–9), impudence (v 9; Exod 17:3, 7) and ingratitude (v 10; Exod 15:24) are all to be renounced. The reference to idolatry, self-indulgence and immorality are very much to the point in view of the problems the Corinthians were having, surrounded as they were by ample opportunity for pagan worship and sensuality. We may not now worship idols so blatantly, but 'if a man's god be that to which he gives all his time and thought and energy, men still worship the works of their own hands more than they worship God' (Barclay). Sensuality and the sexual instinct remain as strong as ever; only a passionate desire for purity can override them, so it is better not to tempt fate. Impudence puts God to the test – consciously or unconsciously, deliberately or unthinkingly, trading on his mercy. 'It'll be OK – God will forgive.' But holiness is as much a part of God as love and mercy.

Paul has already given several hints at the spiritual pride, if not arrogance, that exists in the church at Corinth. Now he backs up his warnings with a reminder of how Israel in the wilderness fell into the same trap (1 Cor 10:12). The experienced traveller located for the night in a strange hotel will check out the fire-escape system before he goes to bed: it's too late to look for it when the alarm bells ring. The same principle applies to us: we should be prepared, whether or not we know we will ever face situations in which we are under pressure to yield to temptation. There always is an 'escape' (v 13), but this promise is not to be invoked as a matter of course. To put ourselves deliberately in the way of temptation, relying on some last-minute 'way of escape' to turn up, is to 'test the Lord' (v 9). Better to avoid temptation altogether, or to at least be ready to resist what we cannot avoid.

An anxious traveller by sea asked the captain if he knew where all the rocks were. When he replied, 'No', the traveller expressed surprise and concern. 'But,' the captain added, 'I know where the deep water is ...' No sensible navigator deliberately sees how close he can go to the rocks. If we look to God in times of temptation, we will find the way through – and he will lead us through it, if we keep close to him. 'Being prepared' is all part of our growth and maturity as believers (9:24–27) and we have no right to expect God to do what we can do for ourselves. In his grace and mercy he will intervene, but that is not to be presumed upon.

For reflection

- In what ways might we make the mistake of 'testing' the Lord (1 Cor 10:9)?

- Can you find examples in the Bible of how the promise of 1 Corinthians 10:13 has been fulfilled? Are there times in your own life when this promise has been fulfilled for you?

IDOLS IN DISGUISE

1 Corinthians 10:14 – 11:1

'Therefore' (1 Cor 10:14) suggests that Paul is now about to sum up his teaching of all that Old Testament experience (vs 1–13). And what is that teaching? 'Flee from idolatry'. It is no accident that the line of argument he now takes follows directly on from his application of the warnings given to Israel, to Christians under the new covenant. The great theme of the Old Testament prophets was Israel's sin of idolatry – the principal cause of their exile to Babylon. Paul is obviously using 'idolatry' in its broadest sense, as the common factor in error of all kinds. An example of this comes in his sharp comment in Colossians 3:5 – 'greed, which is idolatry'. Idolatry also comes as the climax of a list of sins – immorality, impurity, lust, evil desires and greed. Idolatry sounds a bit of an anti-climax – blatant sins followed by comparatively harmless self-indulgence. Not so, says the apostle. Lust is idolatry, making a god of sexual indulgence. Greed is idolatry, making a god of our stomachs (Phil 3:19) or our possessions. The love of money is idolatry. Ideas and philosophies, political ideologies or social causes, can all become idols. In short, whoever or whatever, other than God himself, takes the first and dominant place in our thinking, our planning, our lifestyles, our values and priorities.

We have already commented on the fact that paganism still exists today. However, these other examples demonstrate how widespread and persuasive idolatry can be. To avoid it we do not have to give up living our normal lives, running our homes, raising our families, enjoying our hobbies. But it does mean that our love for God and our desire to please him 'in-forms' (literally 'shapes from within') all we do and are. Paul's comprehensive rule of life – 'whatever you do, do it all for the glory of God (1 Cor 10:31) – is the strongest antidote to idolatry – it simply 'squeezes out' all the rivals.

The appeal to 'sensible' people (v 15) to use their judgement is significant, particularly since, in this letter and others, Paul places so much emphasis on the ministry of the Holy Spirit. It reminds us that in deciding the most 'spiritual' of issues – how to deal with the menace of idolatry – human wisdom, which includes common-sense, has its place. The Old Testament prophets did not hesitate to use common-sense thinking to expose the folly of idol-worship in their day (see, for example, Isaiah 44:12–20, with Isaiah's sarcastic exposure of the follies of idol-worship – it could equally well be the language of the convinced secularist)! Straightforward human reason is a powerful weapon and a valid part of the Christian's armoury. We may aim to 'live by the Spirit', but this does not mean that we switch off our minds altogether. Indeed, if we are open to the Spirit and allow him to direct the way we use our minds, the use of our common-sense and our rational faculties becomes part of living by the Spirit. Thus our minds are transformed and renewed (Rom 12:2), increasingly gaining in insight and spiritual discernment.

The ultimate restraint

Paul now deals with the ultimate question faced by Christians in Corinth. It was not whether they should eat the meat offered in sacrifice in the pagan temples; but rather could or should they actually take part in the feasts that were explicitly held under the patronage of a pagan deity. Paul's answer is an unequivocal 'No!' (vs 18–21). Doubtless he remembered – along with the incidents already listed (1 Cor 10: 6–10) – the strong denunciation of Israel and God's reaction (Deut 32:15–21): 'They sacrificed to demons, which are not God ... The Lord saw this and rejected them ... '[They] angered me with their worthless idols'. And because it is the ultimate question, he reminds them of the ultimate restraint – the cross (1 Cor 10:21). The Christian who shares in the Lord's Supper is united to Christ crucified in a very special way and, at the same time, committed to the one 'body' which is the church. Therefore, taking part in idol-worship makes nonsense of his or her Christian profession.

This does not mean that the idol has any reality in itself. However, it is real to its worshippers, and it represents those demonic powers which oppose all Christ stands for in the world. So the 'all things to all men' principle (9:22) cannot be an absolute one: there are limits to the extent to which Christians can enter into other peoples' interests in order to get alongside them and build bridges of understanding. Sharing in their worship is a 'bridge too far'. Paul distinguishes between 'the table of demon-worshippers' and 'the table of demons' (10:21), a distinction which can help us to decide where to draw the line in such matters.

The final question – 'Are we stronger than he?' (v 22) – is best understood in the light of Deuteronomy 32, a favourite Old Testament passage for Paul and apparently much in his mind as he wrote. It is well worth reading alongside this section of 1 Corinthians. The theme of that chapter was Israel's folly in provoking the Lord to jealousy by getting involved with idols. God is the Rock – 'the strong one' as one Jewish version puts it: to provoke him to anger is complete folly. So Paul's question prepares the way for his later assertion that the reason for the Corinthians' physical debilitation is because they are 'sinning against the body and blood of the Lord' (11:27, 30). Those who attempted to dabble in idolatry at the same time as they worshipped the true and living God simply brought down on their own heads the wrath of the 'Stronger than the strong'.

Constrained by the love of Christ

Paul now returns to his theme in chapter 8, that while we have freedom in Christ, we are also his slaves and this places a constraint on our exercising our freedom at the expense of others. As he does so, he makes his own position clearer, insisting more strongly on the need to avoid causing problems for others. He quotes for a second time the watchword of the 'permissive party' at Corinth – 'Everything is permissible' (10:23; see 8:12). This is one of those deceptively convincing statements with which enthusiastic teachers are prone to overwhelm their followers. But Paul is aware that it is not so simple. He is 'fighting on two fronts, with the libertines on the one hand and the ascetics on the other' (F F Bruce). So, on the face of it, the important general principle which he set out earlier (8:1–2) and repeats in verse 24 is contradicted by verses 25–26. Paul is not afraid of living with such tensions when he is caught between two equally valid but paradoxical principles. In this he gives us a model of how to respond to the controversies which emerge from time to time in the church – both about doctrine and about practice. 'Nobody should seek his own good, but the good of others': this reminds us of the example set by the one whose behaviour should determine our behaviour (Phil 2:4-8).

The sequence of thought flows more smoothly if we read straight on from 10:25–26 to the middle of verse 29, and then go back to verses 27–28, thus:

> Eat anything sold in the meat market without raising questions of conscience, for 'The earth is the Lord's, and everything in it.' … For why should my freedom be judged by another's conscience? … If some unbeliever invites you to a meal and you want to go, eat whatever is put before you without raising questions of conscience. But if anyone says to you, 'This has been offered in sacrifice,' then do not eat it, both for

the sake of the man who told you and for conscience'
sake – the other man's conscience, I mean, not yours.

Yet again, a broad general principle – 'If I take part in the
meal with thankfulness, why am I denounced because of
something I thank God for?' (v 30) – is qualified by a special case that calls for restraint (v 28). If our high-princi-
pled behaviour troubles the conscience of another, we
must be ready to adjust to their scruples – hard to do but,
in the end, more rewarding than conflict and wounded
Christians.

Then Paul follows through with the master principle
that must overrule all others – 'whether you eat or drink
or whatever you do, do it all for the glory of God' (v 31).
The principles controlling Christian behaviour are of two
kinds – the absolute, which must never be 'bent'; and the
conditional, which operate as general rules but which are
not inflexible. The mark of a mature Christian is that he
or she is able to identify which is which and to live accord-
ingly. In this we are guided by reason, common-sense and,
above all, by the wisdom that comes from the work of the
Holy Spirit within us. One rule of life with which we can
be sure of never going wrong is to 'follow the example of
Christ (11:1). But if we are to make this rule reality, the
contents of the four Gospels have to become the very warp
and woof of our being.

For reflection

- Do you think that idolatry is easy or hard to spot
  today? Is there anything that you feel you may be in
  danger of allowing to dominate your life?

- How do we decide whether or not a given action is 'to
  the glory of God' (1 Cor 10:31)?

WORSHIP: AN ORDERLY ACTIVITY

1 Corinthians 11:2–34; 14:26–40

Paul lays down two principles that can help us decide what is right and proper in worship:

> When you come together, everyone has a hymn, or a word of instruction, a revelation, a tongue or an interpretation. All of these must be done for the strengthening of the church ...
>
> But everything should be done in a fitting and orderly way.
>
> (1 Corinthians 14:26, 40)

In the light of these, we are better able to distinguish the detailed instructions relating particularly to the situation at Corinth. As, in turn, we try to relate general principles to this detailed teaching regarding the regulation of worship, we have to keep in mind that the apostle is not contradicting himself. And when we apply general principles to our own day, it may mean there are large differences between ours and the Corinthian experience. What is 'fitting and orderly' in one culture may be the opposite in another.

With all the controversies surrounding these (and similar) passages, we are in constant danger of not seeing the wood for the trees. Attempts to deduce detailed and universal doctrine from every sentence of scripture makes the Bible a happy hunting-ground for legalists and authoritarians. But the Bible writers often used metaphor, allegory and rhetoric to communicate truth and were writing from within their own cultural and historical contexts. It is far better for us to note and acknowledge general principles which can be legitimately applied to this and every age.

Thus Paul's statement in verses 11–12 is a balanced and non-sexist statement of principle, parallel in form and content to 7:3–5, with the emphasis on mutual consent. If we find it difficult to reconcile broad principles with more detailed rules, we should remember that there may have been particular cultural factors that, if we knew them, would explain apparent contradictions. However, Paul does take a remarkably relaxed and pragmatic stance in relation to those who disagree with him (1 Cor 11:16). He does not enforce his teaching with the ultimate sanction – 'This is God's law'; instead, 'It's not the way we do it...'

What the statues reveal

Cultural norms in Corinth were mainly the result of Roman rather than Greek influence, since Corinth had been rebuilt as a Roman colony. Paul's prohibition on men wearing head coverings (v 4) may have been directed against the 'jostling for power and authority amongst the leading families in the church at Corinth following Paul's departure' (David Gill). Gill has studied portraits and statuary of New Testament times in old Corinth and found that Roman men functioning as pagan priests were of a higher social status, and they wore a head covering as a mark of that status:

> Inscriptions show that the role of priest within the colony was filled by members of the social elite. Priesthoods, although they were not magistracies, are frequently named alongside other civic positions of authority in public inscriptions ... the picture is one of rival groups, perhaps from different families within the church, who are using their dress to further their ambition to dominate and thus be honoured by those present.
>
> (Gill, *Tyndale Bulletin* 41:2, p 245.)

In the parallel comment about women's head covering (v 10), the word translated 'veil' in KJV and RSV is actually as translated in NIV – 'sign of authority' – not someone's authority over a woman, but her authority in her own right. The Jewish community was never far from Paul's thoughts, and in synagogue services a woman could play no significant part at all. But 'in Christ she received equality of status with men; she might pray or prophesy at meetings of the church (v 5), and her veil was a sign of this new authority' (F F Bruce).

Evidence from the statuary suggests that it was socially acceptable in a Roman colony for women to be seen bareheaded in public. But 'the wearing of the veil said something about a woman's position in society; the lack of it at a meeting of this kind would have been a poor reflection on her husband' (Gill). The basic custom was for men to wear their hair short and women to wear theirs long – a custom confirmed by contemporary portraits, and Paul seems to be urging the Christians not to be unnecessarily different from the society around. It is the 'decently and in order' principle (14:40) applied to personal appearance.

Praying and prophesying – a shared ministry

It is significant that while much attention has been focused on the headgear of the sexes (11:4–5), little is said about the way Paul accepts that both men and women can and do both 'pray and prophesy' in the church. This is another general truth, though we may find it difficult to reconcile with 14:34–36. Perhaps we should quote Bengel's comment on this passage (Bengel's 'Gnomon' was the commentary on which Wesley based his *Notes on the New Testament*). He found it necessary to say:

> Could we now consult the apostle Paul, while he would not compel those [men] who wear wigs to cast them off, he would decidedly recommend those who have not yet begun the habit to leave them alone for ever, as anything but becoming to men, and especially to men who pray.

But wigs were the fashion in Bengel's day, and eighteenth-century culture made an issue of something which was irrelevant to Corinth and is irrelevant to us. Furthermore, if we take wigs into account, verse 5 becomes nonsensical. A woman might wear a glamorous blonde wig of a kind calculated to disturb the saintliest members of the opposite sex and still claim that she was fulfilling the letter of the law. The pattern of creation (11:12) makes it quite clear that there are purposeful and significant differences between the sexes, and the Christian task is to draw them out to the full (not denying or suppressing them) and then blend them in loving mutual submission to the One from whom 'everything comes'.

From all this worry over what each of the sexes wears on their heads, we can draw the fundamental principle that male-female relationships involve interdependence which implies some degree of equality. Since men and women depend on each another, issues like superiority, priority, submission and authority become secondary. Whatever happens in the world at large, and however men in the natural order may use their brute strength to oppress and dominate women, 'in the Lord' – in the Christian family of the church – interdependence should govern our relationships.

No and yes

We do not always emphasise as we should that taking part in the Lord's Supper is saying a significant 'No' as well as a 'Yes'. Holy Communion is an act of separation as well as showing devotion to Christ. One baptismal liturgy speaks of renouncing 'the world, the flesh, and the devil', and each time we take the bread and wine we renew this pledge of renunciation that formed part of our coming to faith. If we are not ready to renounce evil, we should not receive the bread and wine. As Paul says, the two are incompatible (10:21).

Paul returns to the subject of the Lord's Supper, with a

revealing comment – 'your meetings do more harm than good...' (11:17). When a church gets to such a point, as sometimes happens, it is time to call a halt to give people time to reflect on what they are doing and, possibly, to call in an independent third party who can help them understand what is actually happening. The meal Paul refers to at Corinth was a common meal, a 'love-feast' where the church members shared in 'the Lord's Supper', a specific act of worship focusing on the dying love of the Lord Jesus Christ. It was designed to express, among other things, the unity in Christ of all believers – rich and poor, influential and humble. This was to be supremely evident when they shared the symbols of Christ's sacrifice; as one has said, 'At the cross the ground is level'.

Some arrogant Christians at Corinth were so blind to the truth that they refused to mix with others in the love-feast, began eating before everyone had arrived, and fed themselves greedily while others went hungry. Yes, says Paul, they may go through the motions, but this is not the Lord's Supper, however correctly they observe the tradition. There is no automatic blessing to be had in performing the rites and ceremonies of the Christian faith – we should note God's warning to Israel: 'When you spread out your hands in prayer, I will hide my eyes from you; even if you offer many prayers, I will not listen' (Isaiah 1:15).

As so often in his letter (eg 1 Cor 8:11), Paul returns to the cross to shame the culprits. In doing so, he gives us the earliest recorded account of the central Christian sacrament which is such a vivid reminder of that cross (10:23–26). The words 'was betrayed' are literally 'was being betrayed', suggesting that the whole of Christ's passion, and not merely the incident in Gethsemane, involved a 'betrayal' (see also Jesus' parable of the vineyard, Mark 12:1–12). And 'remembrance' signifies much more than simply recalling the facts of the crucifixion. Just as in the Passover feast the Jews 're-lived' their forefathers' experiences at the Red Sea, so we enter deeply into our Lord's sufferings and passion. In a sense we experience Paul's tremendous statement, 'I have been crucified with Christ' (Gal 2:20). When we take the bread and wine, we are 'recognising the body of the Lord' (1 Cor 11:29), that is, becoming aware of the unity we have with our fellow-believers, wherever they are. We see the body of Christ broken and bleeding on the cross. We also see his 'body' incorporated in the worldwide family of faith, waiting 'until he comes' again. The selfish behaviour of some of the Corinthians was a denial of the unity of the body of believers.

Verses 27–32 make a point which is increasingly being understood and accepted in the world of healing and medicine, that the human being is a single entity of body, mind and spirit. These interact with each other, for good or ill, and it is folly to imagine that we can play fast and loose with any one area of our being and leave the others unaffected. Serious as it was to come under God's judgement, this did not mean their salvation was at stake (see 9:27): rather 'we are being disciplined so that we will not be condemned with the world' (11:32). Even those who died because they had failed to 'recognise the body' were described as 'fallen asleep', a term Paul uses only for believers.

For reflection

- 'Therefore whoever eats the beard or drinks the cup of the Lord in an unworthy manner ...' (1 Cor 11:27).

    How might we take Communion 'in an unworthy manner' today?

- What is the connection between these two verses:

    'For God is not a God of disorder but of peace' (1 Cor 14:33).

    'But everything should be done in a fitting and orderly way' (1 Cor 14:40).

THOSE TROUBLESOME GIFTS: THE GENERAL RULE

1 Corinthians 12:1–30

In their letter to him, the Corinthian church appear to have put a number of questions to Paul on the subject of 'spiritual gifts'. From the way he responds to these, it seems that they were especially concerned about the use and control of the somewhat spectacular gift of 'tongues' – speaking in unknown languages. Paul does not actually use the word 'gifts' in verse 1; the Greek expression mean 'spiritual things' or 'spiritual people', or just 'spirituals'.

Perhaps the Corinthians felt the need to 'compete' with the idol-temples. In excitable Corinth, where tongues-speaking, healing and prophecies all featured in pagan worship, it was natural that this would be a focus of interest, even though 1 Cor 14:23 suggests the kind of problem it may have created in an attention-seeking community. Paul's first response is revealing: it is not how men say things, it is *what* they say that counts. Saying something in 'tongues' does not mean that the words are necessarily significant; they may even be blasphemous (12:3). In particular, the real test is what kind of witness it bears to Jesus. We should note that every true believer is 'gifted' in that he or she can say 'Jesus is Lord', and this is impossible without the Holy Spirit.

Implicit in verse 6 is the Christian doctrine of the Trinity – the Spirit, the Lord (Jesus) and God (the Father). We should keep a proper balance in the way we relate to each person of the Godhead, and be particularly alert to the tendency to confuse their ministries or over-emphasise one at the expense of the others. Human pride and vanity frequently stress the differences, thus provoking divisions within the church. Behind all the various manifestations of the Spirit is the unifying purpose of God – which includes the Father and the Son. This is the one objective test by which we can judge whether or not the Spirit of God is at work in any given situation. The unity of the Godhead should be reflected in the unity of his people.

Gifts are for the common good

Spiritual gifts are 'for the common good': they are not intended to boost the egos of individuals, nor do they guarantee a person's spiritual maturity. As is evident throughout this epistle, 'gifted' members of the church, 'baptised by one Spirit' (v 13) could still, nevertheless, be involved in serious spiritual failure.

The expression 'baptised in the Spirit', widely used nowadays, needs to be properly understood. John the Baptist promised that Jesus would baptise in the Spirit (Mark 1:8), and this was fulfilled at Pentecost (Acts 2:33). Later, it is further fulfilled in the so-called 'Gentile Pentecost' in the home of Cornelius (Acts 11:1–17). In both cases, it relates to a community experience rather than an individual one, an experience which marked a new beginning for the church. The word 'by' (1 Cor 12:13) is best understood as 'in'. It is not that the Spirit does something to us, but rather that we are incorporated into the new covenant people of God, inaugurated at Pentecost, which was a once-for-all definitive act of God. The individual experience of the Spirit is defined in terms of 'drinking' (John 4:14; 7:37–39), and this again is an inward experience, a continuing daily process as we are spiritually nourished and renewed – nothing dramatic or spectacular need happen. Baptism is an outward and visible sign, one of the formal, sacramental elements of Christianity. 'Drinking' emphasises the internal and individual work of the Spirit in us. The fact is that the Christian life is intended to be saturated in the Spirit – outside and in, collectively and individually.

You, however, are controlled not by the sinful nature but by the Spirit, if the Spirit of God lives in you. And if anyone does not have the Spirit of Christ, he does not belong to Christ. But if Christ is in you, your body is dead because of sin, yet your spirit is alive because of righteousness. And if the Spirit of him who raised Jesus from the dead is living in you, he who raised Christ from the dead will also give life to your mortal bodies through his Spirit, who lives in you.

(Romans 8:9–11)

Gifts are the gift of God

'He gives them to each one' (1 Cor 12:11; Heb 2:4). The basic truth about a genuine gift is that it is totally at the discretion of the giver. If the receiver has any part in the process, or in any way tries to prompt the giver to give the gift, it becomes a transaction not a gift. Thus to 'claim' a gift is a contradiction in terms. This does not mean that we should be passive and simply wait for something to happen – later Paul urges us to 'eagerly desire' the best gifts (12:31). But it does warn us against trying to anticipate or manipulate the working of the Holy Spirit.

The list of gifts (vs 7–11) is significant. F F Bruce suggests that Paul sets them down in 'descending order of value' and puts 'tongues' last as a way of rebuking the Corinthians' unhealthy interest in such striking phenomena. If this is so, then he gives priority to 'wisdom' and 'knowledge', the least striking and the most rational of the gifts. Here 'faith' is obviously something other than saving faith without which no one is a Christian. It seems, rather, to be a reference to special endowments of faith given for special purposes.

George Muller of Bristol recorded many miraculous interventions of God in the way food and other necessities were provided for his children's homes. He always maintained that his was not a special 'gift' of faith – it was the same as that of any other believer. But the facts suggest otherwise, and there have been other individuals in the life of the Christian Church who seemed to have a gift of a specially strong faith which works through believing prayer to bring about extraordinary results. But, as Paul emphasises, the wide variety of gifts is an outworking of a fundamental unity of purpose – the overruling of the Holy Spirit, without whom nothing can happen.

The game needs a referee

It calls for a high degree of spiritual maturity for us to be able to distinguish between our natural abilities and the gifts of the Spirit – hence the inclusion of the gift of 'discernment'. In some ways this is the most important of all the gifts. A football referee scores no goals, but he is the most important person on the field: the game would be chaos without him. There was a time when church organs used to be pumped by hand, by an assistant who was hidden behind a curtain on the opposite side to the organist. At a recital, one organist acknowledged several rounds of applause and then, with a flourish, announced, 'Now I will play you an encore.' But nothing happened. After a pause, a voice was heard from the other side of the organ: 'Say "we"!'

There are two excesses to be avoided when discussing the role of the Holy Spirit:

- Verses 14–20: when the Spirit is powerfully and evidently at work, and when much is being made of the gifts of the Spirit, especially the more obvious and dramatic ones, some will be tempted to say, 'I don't have the experiences and abilities that others have. Therefore I can't really be a member of the body of Christ.' Or 'If I am a member of the body of Christ, I don't really count for much.' For these people, Paul has words of encouragement: as a part of the human anatomy, the foot is not as elegant, flexible and useful as the hand – but the body wouldn't get far without it!

- Verses 21–26: on the other hand, others may become so puffed up with self-importance and egoism that they (unconsciously, no doubt!) feel they are the ones that matter in the church, and they don't really need the other, more ordinary characters. However, there is a basic equality of status in God's family: we are all 'slaves of Jesus Christ' (1 Cor 7:22). Alongside this equality of status should go a basic equality of concern for one another (12:25).

Paul is laying the foundation for his teaching in chapter 13 about the removal of all ugly divisions. At first sight, verses 27–30 might be seen as a repetition of what he has said already, but they advance his teaching in several ways. He deals with those ministry gifts which contribute directly to the planting and growth of the church, and then puts them in order of importance – 'apostles, prophets, teachers', etc, with 'tongues' again at the bottom. He emphasises that it is God who appoints his servants according to their gifts: they are not self-appointed.

The metaphor of the church as Christ's body illustrates very beautifully the 'unity in diversity' theme that runs right through this chapter. Even more powerful is the way this metaphor enforces the pattern of interdependence by which the body lives. An invisible failure in some organ buried deep in the body can reduce the whole elaborate system to impotence. The brain itself, that incredibly complex centre of life and thought, depends throughout on tiny 'factories' producing highly complex and rare chemicals. Interdependence is the body's way of life – and the church's too.

A metaphor too far

However, the 'body of Christ' concept has been seriously misinterpreted. It has been taken literally, so that the church is said in some way to be carrying on the incarnation of Christ and actually standing in his place in the world, speaking his words and working his works. This view invests what is a very much human institution with the power and authority that rightly belong to God alone. That Paul was writing to the church at all should make it very clear that the New Testament church fell far short of being in any sense a substitute for her perfect Lord. And our own church today is far from perfect. Taking metaphors literally is a sure way of 'wresting the Scripture to our own destruction' (2 Pet 3:16).

For reflection

- A commentator says, 'In 12:1–3 Paul is clearly implying that part of the trouble in the church at Corinth was the result of members not having broken completely with their pagan past.'

    Is this the case? Can you find evidence for this in Paul's letter?

    In what ways is the church today affected by its members' past lives?

- There are various gifts of the Spirit listed in 12:7–11, but they all have one thing in common. What is it? And how does it help us to assess what in the church is of God and what is not?

- In 1 Corinthians 12:7–11, the apostle lists the different gifts of the Spirit. And verses 27–28 give a list of those whose gifts qualify them to serve the church. But the second list does not include all the gifts listed in the first. Does this mean that some of the gifts in the first list are not for general use? Check them through.

    Think about your own gifts and spend some time in prayer, thanking God for them.

Note

Some have suggested that chapter 13 was originally intended by Paul to be the closing part of his letter, and that chapters 14 and 15 were 'second-thought' endings, prompted partly by the arrival of fresh information about the troubles in the church at Corinth. One scholar says, '1 Corinthians 14 bears all the marks of being spontaneous additions to the material in chapters 12, 13. Chapter 15:1–34 on the resurrection is a classic Pauline pattern. Its structure is a small-scale version of Colossians and the prime pattern of Ephesians. It is understandable that on a subject like resurrection, Paul would have his views well formed and ready to be inserted in a letter at a suitable point...'

So I am deferring detailed study of chapter 13 to the end of this volume. Paul's great call to the way of Christian love makes a fitting climax to this epistle, which has shown throughout how desperately the church at Corinth needed to revise its priorities. That chapter's restraining truth needs to be seen as the ultimate answer to the problems underlying chapters 12 and 14, and its 'here-and-now' relevance is an important corrective to any excitement that might be generated by the glories anticipated in chapter 15. And what more fitting closing statement than 13:13?

> And now these three remain: faith, hope and love.
> But the greatest of these is love.

THOSE TROUBLESOME GIFTS: THE PARTICULAR PRINCIPLES

1 Corinthians 14:1–25

A traveller gets up in the morning, spreads out his map and plans his journey. The road he chooses to follow will be the controlling factor in his day, and it will be either the right or the wrong road. He then gets out his clothing and equipment, and decides what to take with him. These are the secondary factors, and although they are important, they are not fundamental. They are his 'gifts', so to speak. So for the Christian the all-important issue is his or her 'road' – the way of love. The equipment – the 'gifts' – comes second. The experience of the gifts is exciting, even spectacular, but compared with the way of love it is no more than comparing a firework display with the light of the sun. This is how Paul sees it, as he makes clear. Chapter 13 forms the heart of the whole discussion between the end of chapter 12 and the beginning of chapter 14. Loving service of others is not a 'gift': it is in a higher category altogether. It is 'the way'.

As we read chapter 14, it is easy to get bogged down in the details, working out the relative values of 'tongues', 'prophecies', and so on. We know little about how the church at Corinth functioned and what exactly the apostle had in mind while he was writing. But there are a number of clear principles we can draw, and these we can and should take to heart.

Puffed up or built up?

The truth behind all Paul has been saying can be summed up in 8:1b – 'Knowledge puffs up, but love builds up'. 'Building up' is also the controlling theme of chapter 14.

It occurs mostly in variations on the word 'edify' (1 Cor 14:4, 12, 17), and is implied in 'instruct' (v 19) and 'strengthen' (v 26). Paul uses the basic Greek word for 'build' or 'building', and from this we learn that building up its members was the primary purpose for which the church met together. God, through his servants, could clarify and enlarge the church's understanding of the truth and, as a consequence, strengthen the church's faith, enabling them to grow up, to become adults in their 'thinking' (v 20). All through this chapter Paul emphasises the need for right thinking, for the mind to be fully involved in prayer and praise (v 15). The church does not meet just to have an emotionally stimulating time of 'worship'; they meet to be taught by God through his servants. Professor Howard Marshall made a study of what the New Testament reveals about what happened when the early church came together. He writes:

> Worship, so-called, was only one feature of the Christian meeting ... it is a mistake to regard the main, or indeed the only, purpose of Christian meetings as being the worship of God ... the primary element [in the meetings] was the movement from God to man, downward rather than upward ... God comes to his people and uses his human servants to convey his salvation to them, to strengthen and upbuild them...

Certainly this is the emphasis in this chapter. Edifying and strengthening the church is the task of those who lead, and this involves the mind rather than the heart. Any 'feel-good factor' is a bonus: the priority should be given to the 'know-the-truth factor'. As Paul pointed out earlier (2:6–8), the fact that we do not deploy 'the wisdom of the world' does not mean we are simpletons or childish; we have wisdom, too – the wisdom of God – and that demands the full use of our rational faculties. Therefore, not only is 'prophecy' – speaking forth the truth of God – far better for the church than 'tongues', but prophecy itself should be used in a controlled and orderly manner

(14:30, 31) so that the truth can be properly attended to and understood. Verse 16 includes a phrase which suggests an interesting fact about the meetings of the early church. The phrase is literally 'he who occupies the room (or place) of the unlearned'. In verse 24 the 'unlearned' are distinguished from the 'unbelievers', and for their sakes the proceedings should be intelligible and edifying.

Here again there is a scale of values by which to judge the various gifts, and prophecy undoubtedly heads the list; this follows from the principle laid down in 12:7 – 'for the common good' – and Paul's personal preference is quite clear (14:19). But the same principle applies to *all* the gifts, and we must not allow ourselves to be seduced into making our personal satisfaction or fulfilment a measure of our spiritual well-being. In his definition of love in chapter 13 Paul did not include 'love is never self-indulgent', but he might as well have done so. Love should act as an over-all constraint on all we say and do within the Christian community. The tongue is a powerful weapon (James 3:5–12) and can do great good or wreak havoc. Before we let loose our flow of words, we would do well to apply the threefold test (1 Cor 14:3): will what we say strengthen (upbuild), encourage or comfort (console)? If not, why say anything at all?

Necessary controls

Mature discipleship involves the proper use of human reasoning – 'in your thinking be adults' (v 20). It is not a case of human judgement being suspended or overwhelmed by the Spirit's inspiration. Human reason is a gift from God and should be deployed in all our decision-making. A characteristic of childish thinking is irresponsibility. It is no accident that we say 'older *and* wiser' – both qualities should go together.

Another necessary control is to measure what happens against scripture. Paul makes his own appeal to the word of God ('the Law', v 21) to back up his argument, reminding the Corinthians of an episode in the life of Isaiah, who warned the people that if they refused to listen to what

God was saying, they would hear some very unwelcome 'tongues' – the voices of foreign invaders, though even this would only harden them in their rebellion.

Finally, all that goes on when the church is meeting for worship is to be done in 'a fitting and orderly way' (v 40). This could be seen as a very 'uninspired' way of responding to God, but only if the spiritual validity of God-given wisdom and judgement is discounted – which it should never be. The worship can, of course, include contributions from individuals – songs, a word or a revelation (v 26), but these contributions should not be given in a chaotic or competitive manner. Verse 31 suggests that the gift of prophecy was very widely distributed around the congregation at Corinth. Paul insists that the prophets are responsible for the use of their gift and, again, that the basic principle of peace rather than disorder must be observed.

One last thing to note: in one of the earliest Greek texts the phrase 'in all the congregations of the saints' (v 33) is attached to the preceding sentence and followed by a full stop. So the verse reads: 'For God is not a God of disorder but of peace, as in all the congregations of the saints.' And verses 34 and 35 follow verse 40. Read this way, it becomes easier to regard the teaching in verses 34 and 35, that women should remain silent during the meetings, as arising from the particular circumstances of the church at Corinth.

For reflection

• 'In the church I would rather speak five intelligible words to instruct others than ten thousand words in a tongue' (1 Cor 14:19). What are the limitations to speaking in tongues outlined in this chapter?

  What place does Paul give to the use of rational judgement in contrast to speaking in tongues (see also vs 9, 15–16, 20)?

• Do you think an unbeliever coming into a church will be convicted by prophecy (1 Cor 14:24–25)? Has this happened in your experience?

THE HEART OF THE MATTER

1 Corinthians 15:1–11

The elders have called the whole congregation together to hear his letter read out. They become very subdued as they listen to him rebuking them for behaviour they had been careful not to report. Some are angry. How dare he? Who does Paul think he is? Others are alarmed. Is it too late to change? What can be done? Paphros is experiencing mixed feelings – anxiety at the prospect of being thrown out of the church, but anguish at any thought of separation from his Julia. Those who know Paul personally may sense his real concern for the church coming through the voice of the reader. However, towards the end there is a stir of excitement, triggered by that little word 'Now' (15:1). Surely the apostle has something encouraging and exciting to tell them as he nears the end of his letter! He has outlined their divisions and quarrels, their tolerance of immorality, their abuse of the Lord's Supper, their all-absorbing interest in the spectacular. But now...

What is Paul's prescription for this sick church? 'The gospel', which they had received way back in the beginning of the church (2:2) – 'Jesus Christ and him crucified'.

Of course! This is what we're all about. This is what we have lost sight of. It is the gospel which creates a healthy church, and the gospel which heals a sick church. At the heart of this gospel is the crucified Saviour and risen Lord. The cross (1:18) not only has the power to save the unbeliever, but also the power to heal the broken and strained relationships that lie at the heart of the church's problems.

Truth beyond discussion

There is no uncertainty about what this gospel is: Paul sets it out in plain language – Jesus Christ, crucified and risen; a person, not a system; a Saviour, not a political leader; a living Redeemer, not a hero from the past. It is all too easy to marginalise this basic message as we allow the world to dictate the church's agenda and try to adjust the gospel to suit. As Paul has pointed out already in chapter 2, if there is any adjusting to be done it is the world which must adjust its so-called 'wisdom' to the apparent 'foolishness' of the gospel. Moreover, the gospel is defined 'according to the Scriptures': the meaning of Christ's death is mirrored in the whole sacrificial system of the Old Testament, reflected in the frequent New Testament references to the 'Lamb' of God; the meaning of Christ's sacrifice as an atonement for sin is foreshadowed in the prophets – he died in our place and for our sin (Isaiah 53:4–6). This message may be labelled 'foolishness' by the world, but it is still the life-changing power of God.

The gospel is embodied in one total 'event': death-plus-resurrection, cross-plus-empty tomb (1 Cor 15:3–5). It is not difficult to see why. Without the resurrection, the cross would have been a futile act of self-sacrifice; without the cross, the resurrection would have been no more than an awesome but meaningless demonstration of God's power. Paul describes the appearances of the risen Lord in some detail because the resurrection is the clinching evidence that Jesus is indeed the Son of God, and therefore has authority to do all that is being claimed for him.

However, Paul was never content to discuss the gospel purely in theoretical or theological terms, any more than we should be. 'Do you want an example of what the gospel can do?' he asks. 'Then look at me!' (v 10). As a Pharisee he had been bitterly prejudiced against Jesus, that upstart preacher from Galilee. As a scholar he had despised the naiveté of this unsophisticated carpenter with his homespun parables. As a patriot he had had no time for turning the other cheek to brutal Roman soldiery, even if he was not himself a terrorist. All this was swept away in one overwhelming moment of truth when he was confronted with the living Lord Jesus. Note how he puts the changes in himself as a person before he talks about what he has achieved. 'I am what I am' comes before 'I worked harder than all of them' (vs 9–11).

The great temptation in Christian service is to focus attention on achievements. Although this may reflect 'the spirit of the age', this is the reverse of what God is looking for in us. Too many outstanding 'achievers' in the Christian church have ended up betraying the cause by failures in their personal lives. The threefold repetition of the word 'grace' shows where Paul is putting the emphasis: it was through the grace of God that he became a believer; it was through the grace of God that he has become the effective apostle he is. Paul is humble enough to regard himself as 'one abnormally born' (v 8), the 'last' of the apostles to whom Christ in his mercy had given the task of bearing his message of grace. The gospel involves a kind of transformation: the shifting of a person's centre of gravity from self to Christ. If this change is not happening, the church – however busy, however impressive, however socially conscious – is not doing its job.

For reflection

- Look through the points that Paul considers are the essential truths of the gospel (1 Cor 15:3–5). What is the special importance of the words 'was buried' (v 4) and 'appeared' (vs 5–7)?

- Paul attributes his effectiveness to 'the grace of God', but then goes on straightaway to say, 'I worked harder than all of them' (1 Cor 15:10).

  Is there a contradiction here? How can the grace of God be held in balance with a person's achievements? Which does Paul seem to regard as the more important? Can you see where God's grace has been operating in your own life?

THE FOUNDATION FACT OF FAITH

1 Corinthians 15:12–58

The Greeks believed in life after death, but in the limited form of the 'immortality of the soul' – a shadowy existence in a kind of ghostly underworld. Christianity goes further than this, promising a 'resurrection of the body' – though not in grossly materialistic terms, as Paul later makes plain (15:42–44). But it certainly implies a self that is recognisably the same individual who lived and died on earth. This continued existence all stems from the bodily resurrection of Jesus himself. The resurrection appearances of Jesus give us a clue to our own. He was recognisable, yet very different; he seemed to be living in a different dimension – one where the spiritual realm and the physical world could perceive and interact with each other in a more direct way that they do in this one.

Christ's resurrection rounded off his work on the cross in offering himself as a sacrifice for sin. He has fought and conquered death, and this offering had been accepted and ratified by God. Paul stresses that if Jesus had not risen from the dead, two things would have followed:

- The gospel message the apostles were preaching was 'empty' (v 14) – it had no solid core of truth. It was just one more speculation to put alongside the philosophies and cults of the Graeco-Roman world.

    But the gospel is rooted and grounded in historical fact, not in human speculation. It is this that distinguishes it from virtually every other religion, ideology and mythology.

- The gospel message was both useless and baseless (v 17). It could achieve nothing worthwhile.

   But what had transformed Paul's life was an encounter with a living being risen from the dead. 'Who are you, Lord?' The reply? 'I am Jesus' (Acts 9:5): two short sentences establishing a personal relationship in the here-and-now, an encounter that is the essence of the message. No other religion or philosophy can make this claim.

A hard question to answer

People do not knowingly give 'false witness' (1 Cor 15:15) without some powerful reason or some personal gain in view. But if we ask the question 'What did Paul and the other apostles gain from their witness to the risen Lord?', the answer has to be 'Nothing but sacrifice, suffering, hardship and death' (see 2 Cor 4:7–12; 6:3–10). Why did they persist?

The gospel is not simply an introduction to a new way of living life on earth: it brings with it the promise of eternity, of escape from sin and victory over death (1 Cor 15:17; Heb 2:14–15). This is only possible because of Christ's pioneering work, his conquering the grave and opening 'the kingdom of heaven to all believers'. If this work was proved to be untrue, if Christ had done nothing on our behalf, if nothing lies beyond the grave, then believers are indeed to be pitied (1 Cor 15:19): we remain enmeshed in sin and its consequences, trapped in this life of separation from God, the source of life, liberty and true joy (v 19). What dupes to give up our entire lives, often at great cost, on a false premise.

We often want to know what Jesus Christ can do for us in the here-and-now. Isn't he the answer to all our problems, the secret of peace of mind? Won't he deliver us from anxiety, bring about social justice and prosperity? But in focussing on this we are shifting the centre of gravity of our faith. Becoming a Christian may or may not benefit our lives in this world, but this should not be the only reason for faith. We believe the gospel because we know it is true, because we are convicted of our need to be put right with God, because knowing Jesus is like holding in our possession a pearl of great price (Matt 13:44–46). Being a Christian in the world today may leave us at a disadvantage, but what sustains us is the freedom of living under Christ's law and the hope of resurrection to eternal life in God's kingdom of love and peace. If our hope is without foundation, we would indeed be fools to follow the Lord Jesus Christ.

True by every test

One way to demonstrate that something is true is to point out the grim consequences if it is not. This has been the thrust of Paul's defence of the resurrection (1 Cor 15:12–19). However, at verse 20 he moves over to the positive and sets out the certain consequences of the well-proven fact of the resurrection (vs 3–7, 20–28). We should note that just as the negative consequences (no resurrection equals no salvation) are absolute and inevitable, so also are the positive consequences. The resurrection authenticates the full and demanding claims of Jesus Christ upon all humankind, and we must respond. The cross and the empty tomb leave no room for the idea that 'all roads lead to God'. The resurrection is nothing or it is everything: there is no middle ground. Therefore, far from being a minor local incident in an obscure Roman province, the bodily resurrection of Jesus is the very hinge of history, the turning point in time that opens the way for the end of time itself and the final and absolute triumph of God's kingdom.

Verses 21–28 set out one of the most significant statements in the whole Bible – a brief history of humanity from the creation to the final glory. It is primarily about the people of God (Israel), but finally involves the whole human race. Successive key events outline the broad sweep of God's plan, and it all stems from the resurrection of Jesus – the sin of Adam and Eve, the coming of Jesus

Christ, his death and resurrection, the return of Jesus Christ and the resurrection of his people, the establishment of his kingdom, the final defeat of sin and death, and the establishment of God as sovereign over all in everlasting glory. The idea that all humankind is involved in Adam's disastrous disobedience (v 22) is dealt with more fully elsewhere (Rom 5:12–19). If we are tempted to think this unfair, we should remind ourselves that it is this same principle of identification with a given individual – that is, Jesus Christ – which makes it possible for us to be forgiven and redeemed, because we have all added our personal quota to the sum total of humanity's sin and folly.

Paul is led inevitably from the personal consequences of the resurrection to Christ's total cosmic triumph (1 Cor 15:24). In spite of appearances in this chaotic world of disaster, conflict and folly, God is moving steadily towards his intended goal.

'I die every day'

Quite suddenly the centre of interest shifts from God to man (vs 29–34). Regarding the problem of the baptism for the dead, Leon Morris remarks in his commentary on 1 Corinthians that 'between 30 and 40 explanations have been suggested for it, and we cannot traverse them all.' However, note Paul's declaration – 'I die every day' (v 31; Gal 2:20). On the 'surface' it relates to the way he is laying his life on the line every day for Christ. But he accepts physical danger because he has laid himself on the line at a deeper level – he has 'died' to self and is totally given over to serving his Lord and Master.

'Dying to self' is a basic tenet of evangelical teaching on holiness, and an essential element in Christian spirituality. The counselling movement with its emphasis on 'loving oneself' and 'proper self-worth' has tended to blunt the edge of this demanding doctrine. In the search for fulfilment, the encouragement of 'self-awareness' and the emergence of 'assertiveness training', we may have lost sight of a vital ingredient of biblical faith. If we want to create space for the living Lord to work in our lives by his Spirit, something like 'dying to self' surely has to happen.

It is interesting to see how modern developments bring new meaning to old writings. The modern medical usage of the word 'scan' has given new force to the Victorian hymn writer's couplet: 'Thy kind but searching glance can scan/The very wounds that shame would hide' (referring to the way Christ sees into our lives). Jesus describes the result of his 'scan' of the human heart in plain language – 'evil thoughts, murder, adultery, sexual immorality, theft, false testimony, slander. These are what make a man "unclean" ' (Matt 15:19–20). There must be a radical change of heart if there is to be any hope of spiritual progress. Paul describes this change as nothing less than a 'death' (to self-will) and a 'new creation' (2 Cor 5:17). We identify ourselves so closely with Jesus in his death that it is as if we died with him to our old way of life and rose with him to a new.

What the philosophers could not understand

The abrupt command – 'stop sinning' (1 Cor 15:34) – is probably directed at the 'permissive' faction in the church at Corinth who were taking the promise of God's forgiveness too far. They probably considered themselves more enlightened than others, free to indulge their carnal appetites: 'Let us eat and drink, for tomorrow we die' (v 32). But, Paul says, 'Bad company corrupts good character', and they are really demonstrating the fact that they are 'ignorant of God'.

Then at verse 35, the apostle turns to deal with another group. The idea of a general and bodily resurrection made possible by the resurrection of Jesus Christ would strike the Greek intellect as wildly implausible. The obvious objection a thoughtful Greek would make to the doctrine of the resurrection would be that it was quite clear and provable that after death the human body decayed or was destroyed. Paul's response is direct and sharp. The NIV's rendering, 'How foolish' is too gentle (v 36). What he actually writes is 'You foolish man...' He not only answers the objection, but points to the wonder of life and the infinite power of God, life's author.

A walk in the countryside in the autumn, when the newly sprouting winter wheat covers the dark soil with a delicate film of green, uplifts the soul with its vivid reminder of the miracle of life out of death. The illustration of the seed (v 37), which dies and disappears until it springs into a new growth, suggests how a new 'spiritual' body might take the place of the old physical one and points us to the power of God to transform all things. Just as the central theme of the cross (love sacrificing itself for others) is built into Christian living, so also the central truth of resurrection is the core – life out of death, hope out of despair, gain out of loss, glory out of shame. Jesus himself applied it to his own suffering and death (John 12:24): Paul now extends it to all believers. The analogy of sowing the seed and the springing up of new life is a master-stroke of inspiration, for it uses the familiar and fundamental principle by which all life is sustained to illustrate the way in which we will ultimately be transformed from the earthly to the heavenly realm. The final resurrection – 'being clothed with our heavenly body' (2 Cor 5:1–4) – is the necessary and inevitable climax of God's work demonstrated so unmistakably by the empty tomb and Jesus' Easter appearances.

> And if the Spirit of him who raised Jesus from the dead is living in you, he who raised Christ from the dead will also give life to your mortal bodies through his Spirit, who lives in you.
>
> (Romans 8:11)

> I lay in dust life's glory dead
> And from the ground there blossoms red
> Life that shall endless be...
> (G Matheson)

The climax of history

Paul's teaching about death and resurrection reaches its climax (1 Cor 15:52): the last trumpet, the emptied graves, transfigured lives. Paul reveals a 'mystery' (v 51; 1 Thess 4:13–17) – what will happen to those who are alive at the Second Coming. They will be 'changed', given a new quality of life which will enable them to share in the eternal glory with those who had died but have now been raised to life. Verse 56 puts the whole matter of death in its proper context: it is not the physical pain or the emotional strain or the sense of loss that makes death so hard to contemplate; the real sting of death is *sin*. Modern medicine and the hospice movement have done much to alleviate the physical and mental discomforts of dying. But sin cannot be so readily disposed of. We are brought back to the basic truth of the gospel – 'Christ died for our sins' (1 Cor 15:3). Many believers have found peace in their dying through their trust in Christ crucified and risen. This is dramatic and exciting truth, a desperately needed vision of hope in a sick and broken world. The question then arises, How do we respond to this prospect of a returning Lord?

Some are fascinated by the prospect of Christ's Second Coming and indulge in endless speculation about the how and when of it. Recently a well-known American radio preacher had to retract his forecast that Jesus Christ would return 'between September 15th and 27th 1994'. Such speculation is guaranteed to attract followers and breed cynics.

By saying 'we' (v 51), Paul puts himself among those who will be alive when Jesus returns (as he does in 1 Thess 4:15, 17). But in a later reference (2 Cor 4:13 – 5:10) he sees himself among those who have died and will be 'raised with Jesus'. Living or dead, we will experience the greatest reunion of all time. While we can praise God for such a hope (1 Cor 15:57), even more emphatically, we are called to buckle down to the daily task of living for

God (v 58). This may seem like an anti-climax – death swallowed up in victory, sin nullified, mortal clothed with immortality. 'Therefore, my dear brothers, stand firm. Let nothing move you. Always give yourselves fully to the work of the Lord...' Is that all? Yes, and it is more than enough. The timing of Christ's Second Coming is God's responsibility: the task of living in the light of this expectation is ours. Since we do not know the time (Matt 24:36) we must get on with it. As C S Lewis points out:

> If you read history you will find that the Christians who did most for this present world were just those who thought most of the next. The apostles themselves, who set on foot the conversion of the Roman Empire, the great men who built up the Middle Ages, the English evangelicals who abolished the slave trade, all left their mark on earth because their minds were occupied with heaven. Aim at heaven and you will get earth thrown in ... aim at earth and you will get neither.

For reflection

- 'If only for this life we have hope in Christ, we are to be pitied more than all men' (1 Cor 15:19).

  Some of the emphasis in the church nowadays is on what Jesus can do for us now – personal fulfilment, social justice, community care, and so on. How does this fit in with Paul's powerful statement and with verse 58? How can we achieve a balance?

- Clear thinking ('Come back to your senses', 1 Cor 15:34) and correct knowledge ('some are ignorant of God') are said to be the antidote to sinning. How do you think this fits with statements like Romans 8:13 which emphasise the role of the Holy Spirit?

TYING UP THE LOOSE ENDS

1 Corinthians 16:1–18

'Now about the collection for God's people...' Verse 1 brings us down to earth with a bump! What a prosaic subject to come so soon after that stirring review of the tremendous events awaiting humankind at the end of the age! But it confirms the point already made (15:58): whatever the future held for Paul and his friends, there were believers in Jerusalem who were going hungry, and the younger churches of the Empire could help to meet their need. This was a 'Tear Fund' type mission from Antioch to Jerusalem, which preceded the first sending out of missionaries (Acts 11:29; 13:1; Rom 15:25–28). There is here no hint of any dichotomy between 'social responsibility' and 'preaching the gospel' which has so often caused divisions and bitterness between fellow believers. Just as Jesus ministered to body and soul, so Christians who share his vision of human need should share his practical compassion as well as his spiritual burden. 'Therefore, as we have the opportunity, let us do good to all people, especially to those who belong to the family of believers' (Gal 6:10).

Paul insists on making careful, practical arrangements, so that the donors will have a full share in the process and so that there could be no question about the way the money was handled (see also 2 Cor 8:19–21). His comment – 'If it seems advisable' (1 Cor 16:4) – is in contrast to his 'if the Lord is willing' (4:19), suggesting a balanced way of decision-making. A practical and prudential assessment of circumstances as seen from the human point of view was a factor in deciding what the Lord wanted him to do. There is a different emphasis in 'if the Lord permits' (16:7). Paul remains sensitive to any change of plan that the Lord might be wanting him to take on board.

The final verses of this chapter give us a glimpse of that all-important network of trusted friends and colleagues which served as Paul's equivalent of a modern missionary organisation. Timothy, Apollos, Stephanas, Fortunatus, Achaicus, Priscilla and Aquila – all very different characters with different gifts, but all deployed skilfully by the apostle and all contributing to the common cause, helping Paul to keep in touch with the young and growing churches scattered around the Mediterranean rim.

The apostle's final word of exhortation, 'Do everything in love' (v 14), is clearly related to the issues he has been dealing with. Doctrinal error, moral laxity and raw selfishness may have slipped through their defences; courage may have failed them when they were called upon to be distinct in a difficult cultural environment. But everything must be steeped in Christlike love. The word 'in' is more important than it might at first seem. Paul does not say 'with love', as if love were something that flavours our acts like spice added to food. It is *in* love – love is to be the total environment within which Christians live and serve, a vivid reminder of chapter 13 to which we now turn as the climax to this experience of New Testament Christianity.

For reflection

- Note the careful arrangements (1 Cor 16:4; 2 Cor 8:16 – 9:5) Paul makes so that there could be no question about the way money was handled and distributed. Does this have anything to say to churches today?

- What does this passage teach us about the way churches should relate to each other? Do our organisations and institutions get in the way? How?

LOVE, THE MASTER KEY

1 Corinthians 13:1-13

In spite of Paul's emphasis on the unity of the body of Christ (12:12 *ff*), his teaching in chapter 12 is inevitably divisive: different gifts are given to different people (13:11); some will get more attention than others; some gifts are spectacular, others humdrum. However, the 'most excellent way' of love (12:31), is available to all without exception. Love is not a gift that some receive and others don't, so we have no excuse for not living out a life of love.

It must be said straight away that the love of which Paul speaks is not something that people can achieve if they would only try hard enough. Human nature tends to have sporadic bursts of enthusiastic altruism, and sustained self-giving of this order is very unusual. But 'God has poured out his love into our hearts by the Holy Spirit' (Rom 5:5). This process involves a radical and fundamental change at the very centre of our being – the will. We 'die' to self-centred living and 'rise' to a new quality of life made possible by Jesus Christ: 'he died for all, that those who live should no longer live for themselves but for him who died for them' (2 Cor 5:15). If we bypass this radical new beginning, we shall end up in a wilderness of frustration and failure.

Verses 1–3 are something of a 'put-down' for the Corinthian church. Their letter had been concerned with morality, divorce and the exciting gifts of the Spirit. But for the apostle, love should have been the most important of all. Without self-giving Christlike love, the most spectacular of the gifts of the Spirit became nothing. 'A Christian community can make shift somehow if the "gifts" of chapter 12 are lacking. It will die if love is absent' (F F Bruce).

The word we must get right

In the Greek world – as in our day – the word 'love' was like debased coinage and therefore needed careful definition. To avoid misunderstanding, the early church had to introduce a new word (*agape*) to differentiate Christian love from the other definitions of love in the Greek vocabulary. As Paul sets out his description of *agape* love, we would do well to stand at the foot of the cross, looking up to Jesus, the embodiment of true love as he 'hung and suffered there' (see 1 John 3:16). Nothing sentimental, nothing glamorous, only a steely determination to give himself away for the sake of others in need. This is the distinctive quality of love as it should be seen in his people – entirely motivated by the selfless intention of the lover, independent of the response, the worth, the attractiveness of the beloved.

First, Paul clears the ground (1 Cor 13:1–3). He gets rid of any suggestion that lack of love can be compensated for by other Christian qualities or activities. It is as if he is dealing with an objector who wants to argue that while *agape* love is very desirable, it is not the only mark of genuine belief. 'Not so,' says the apostle. Then he gives a sharp reminder of the idol-worship from which many of the Corinthian Christians had escaped ('resounding gong and clanging cymbal'): processions of chanting priests accompanied by just such 'sacred' sounds were a feature of temple worship, and the streets of Corinth at times resounded with such empty clangour. 'This meaningless noise,' says Paul, 'is what the gift of tongues in a professedly Christian life adds up to if love is absent.'

'All right,' says the objector. 'What about the gift of prophecy which you yourself rate so much more highly than tongues?' (14:1). 'No,' says Paul. 'Without love, not only is the gift of prophecy worthless; so is the person exercising it – 'I am nothing' (13:2). The same goes for faith, even faith that moves mountains (Mark 11:23). Generosity, even martyrdom, cannot make up for lack of love. We may sum it all up by saying that if we are looking for a reliable indicator of spiritual life, it is not whether we speak in tongues, but whether our tongues 'speak the truth in love' (Eph 4:15). It is not whether we declare the mind of God in prophecy, but whether we communicate the meaning of the love of Christ. It is not whether we move mountains of granite by our faith, but whether we move mountains of suffering by selfless compassion.

Reality, not fantasy

The core of this exposition of true Christian love is in verses 4–8. Paul lists love's qualities – eight negative qualities and seven positive ones, all very direct and practical – the antithesis of the fantasies which are a feature of selfish love and which all too often prove short-lived and disappointing. The first two positive qualities are 'fruits of the Spirit' (13:4a; Gal 5:22): 'Love is patient, love is kind'. The Greek word for 'patient' suggests being patient with *people* rather than with circumstances, a patience which springs from being able to enter into another person's feelings and to understand the conscious and unconscious forces that may be prompting difficult behaviour. Similarly, kindness is a quality which adjusts to another person's ability to cope and does not demand too much too soon.

Then come the eight negative qualities of love (1 Cor 13:4b–6). These are no less important for being negative: defining God's love is something like defining his holiness – it is a case of 'Not this ... Not that ...' Love is a disciplined and well-defined pattern of relationships, observing well-defined boundaries, as ready to say 'No' as 'Yes'.

The first three negatives are related – envy, boasting, pride. They are all the outworking of a person's inner insecurity, self-will and self-concern, ways of boosting one's own ego by denigrating others; they are devices for covering up one's own deficiencies by magnifying the failings of others. When someone is at peace with himself or herself and at peace with God, content to do God's will, the need to cut others down to size or envy them never arises. The word translated 'rude' (v 5) takes in unseemly behaviour of all kinds – the reference is to that kind of uncouth self-assertiveness which ignores others' feelings or deliberately sets out to offend them.

On a broader front, love does not take a depraved pleasure in other people's depravity: it is primarily concerned with truth (v 6). In the great moral issues, love knows where it stands; it is not a 'soft touch', yielding easily to pressure or compromise.

Love will outlast everything

Paul moves to the rest of the positive qualities of love (v 7). J B Phillips renders this verse well: 'Love knows no limit to its endurance, no end to its trust, no fading of its hope. It can outlast anything'. The fourfold 'always' of NIV points to one of love's most important qualities – its consistency. You can rely on *agape* love: it is the truth behind that significant comment about Jesus: 'having loved his own ... he now showed them the full extent of his love' (John 13:1). Though his disciples abandoned and betrayed him, Jesus' love for them never faltered.

'Fails' (1 Cor 13:8) translates the common Greek word for 'falls' or 'is ruined'. On a slight hillock beside the River Bure in Norfolk, a magnificent Benedictine Abbey once stood, towering over the marshes, surrounded by the living quarters and offices of a great monastic centre, all built in durable stone and brick. Today St Benets has all but disappeared: a few lumps of broken stonework, and a gatehouse which has been turned into a windmill, are all that remain. But on the highest piece of ground, where once stood the abbey's high altar, there now stands a tall, plain oaken cross. It stands out against the empty sky – an eloquent testimony of the love that does not collapse into ruin, the love of Christ. Today, around the world, in refugee camps, in remote hospitals, in leprosy centres, in orphanages, in favelas, in famine-stricken villages, this love is still being 'poured out' in practical caring by the servants of Jesus. Unlike the popular media, they do not quickly lose interest and move on to some other sensation.

Love is again compared with the exercise of the 'gifts' (v 8) – tongues, knowledge, prophecy: love is beyond value and will outlast them all. This fact leads Paul to set the discussion within the framework in which his entire life is structured – the promise of Christ's return and the hope of eternity. It was this hope which sustained him when things were going badly and which coloured all his apostolic ministry. In the here-and-now, Paul is an all-action, self-sacrificing missionary. But his heart is in his heavenly homeland (2 Cor 4:13 – 5:5). This world is the 'nursery' where, like children, we rush around, we dream and fantasise, we get excited over trifles. In heaven we shall finally be grown-up; we shall see things as they really are, and the only thing that we shall carry over from this passing world will be love, Christlike love (1 Cor 13:7). Prophecies, tongues, healing, words of knowledge – all the exciting paraphernalia of our earthly spirituality – will be finished.

So we can stop guessing what heaven will be like, and start living the heavenly life in the here-and-now as we live lives of self-giving, self-sacrificing love, above reproach.

For reflection

- In his description of love in 1 Cor 13:5–7, Paul sets out three positive qualities of love and three negative qualities. Why is this, do you think? Does it say something about fallen human nature?

- Looking back over the whole of 1 Corinthians, and bearing in mind what was going on at Corinth when Paul wrote his letter, can you set out those characteristics of his response that could serve as an example of how Christian leadership might deal with a church in trouble?